VENUS & SERENA

My Seven Years as Hitting Coach for the Williams Sisters

VENUS & SERENA

My Seven Years as Hitting Coach for the Williams Sisters

DAVE RINEBERG

Frederick Fell Publishers, Inc.
2131 Hollywood Blvd., Suite 305, Hollywood, FL 33020
Phone: (954) 925-5242   Fax: (954) 925-5244
Web Site: www.FellPub.com

Frederick Fell Publishers, Inc.
2131 Hollywood Boulevard, Suite 305
Hollywood, Florida 33020
954-925-5242
e-mail: fellpub@aol.com
Visit our Web site at www.fellpub.com

Published by Frederick Fell Publishers, Inc., 2131 Hollywood, Blvd., Suite 305,
Hollywood, Florida 33020.

Library of Congress Cataloging-in Publication Data

Rineberg, Dave, 1965-
    Venus & Serena: My 7 Years with the Williams Sisters / by Dave Rineberg.
    p. cm.
    ISBN 0-88391-036-5
    1. Williams, Venus, 1980-2. Williams, Serena, 1981 - 3. Rineberg, Dave, 1965-4.
Tennis players--United States--Biography. 5. African-American women tennis
players--Biography. 6. Tennis coaches--United States--Biography. I. Title.

GV994.A1 R56 2002
796.352'092'273--dc21
[B]

                                    2001054543

10 9 8 7 6 5 4 3 2 1

This Book is for:

My Mom, Barbara, who took me to her tennis games with the ladies and who taught me the most important human characteristic, compassion.

My Dad, Richard, who has always been my hero and who taught me how to compete in sports and life.

My Sister, Charlotte, who I love dearly and without her help this book would never have happened.

My Brothers, Rick and Tom, for all their help and support throughout my athletic career.

Jennifer, not a day goes by girl.

Pat and Jim, for always being there on my road less traveled.

Gary Kraus, for those little life lessons.

MacGyver, the best tennis ball retrieving yellow lab ever.

CONTENTS

ACKNOWLEDGMENTS

This book is filled with the names of people who have come into my life and through my life and made a difference.

For their kind and invaluable assistance, I would like to thank all the players at Frederick Fell Publishers, Inc.:

Publisher Don Lessne, who saw the vision for this book.

Art Director Elena Solis, who put together a Picasso of a book cover.

Graphic Designer and Editor Lora Sindell-Horton, for all her creative help and advice in the book's production.

My sincerest thanks to each one of them.

THE
CALL

I

The phone in the pro shop rang as I was stepping out the door for my 6pm lesson. There was no shop attendant at this time on a Sunday, and I decided to let the answering machine pick up a message. The year was 1992, and at the time, I was working as the head tennis pro at the Deerfield Beach Tennis Center, an eight-court city facility. I had just one more hour to go, before I would be off to Kansas for my Christmas vacation. Although it was relatively cool for a late December day in South Florida, it was still always good to go back home to Kansas and enjoy some really cold winter weather. After finishing my lesson, I raced inside to grab my bag and lock up. As I was about to turn the lock, I noticed the red light on the answering machine blinking. 'The call that came in just before my lesson,' I thought to myself. I propped open the door with my tennis bag and stepped back inside to play the message. It was a man's voice.

"I am calling for Mr. Dave Rinesburg," I was immediately annoyed at the fact that the man could not even say my name correctly and listened disinterestedly to the rest of the message. "I has two daughters that I would like you to coach. Please give me a call at your convenience, Richard Williams."

I scribbled down the name and number and started to put it in my day planner, however a trash can just outside the door caught my eye. I was going on vacation for five days and did not want to be bothered with returning phone calls. I crumbled up the note and did my best Larry Bird imitation, shooting it into the trash can. I locked the door behind me and went home to pack for my Christmas vacation.

My flight was scheduled for 8am the next morning, and I tossed and turned all night in anticipation, as I usually do when I have an early flight the next day. For some reason, my mind kept thinking of that message I had thrown away and of the voice of Richard Williams. The name sounded so familiar. It was 5am when I sat up in bed, Williams! It finally hit me, I realized who he was. I remembered that there were two girls from California that had just moved to the area, and people were beginning to talk about them. I had heard they were tennis phenoms at age ten and eleven and that they were training hard to become professionals. 'I have to call him back,' I thought to myself, but

3

as I reached for my day planner, I remembered my earlier jump shot into the trash can. I looked at my watch. It was now 5:30am and the Deerfield Beach sanitation department picks up the garbage at the tennis shop at 6am. I grabbed my bags and raced out to my car. I got there at 6:15 and just knew that the garbage had been picked up, since the sanitation guys were never late. I ran towards the door, and upon hearing the sound of a truck, I looked to the parking lot to see the sanitation truck just pulling in. They were late! I looked into the trash can to see the crumbled up paper containing the message at the bottom. Two of the men came up as I pulled the paper out and put it safely inside my pocket.

"Can we get the trash real quick? We're kind of behind this morning," one of the men said to me.

"Take it away," I answered, "and you guys have a good holiday." I got back in my car and went to catch my flight. That was an opportunity I had almost missed and I decided I would call Mr. Williams back as soon as my plane landed in Wichita, Kansas.

It was around 9pm by the time I got to a phone. I dialed the number on the waded up piece of paper in my pocket, hoping that it was not too late to be calling. The phone rang and a man answered the phone.

"Hi Mr. Williams, this is Dave Rineberg from the Deerfield Beach Tennis Center. You called me concerning your daughters."

"Yes Mr. Rinesburg. How are you this evening?" He was very polite as he continued, "I hope you don't mind, but I got your name from someone at the Chris Evert Charities office. They said you would be the perfect hitting coach for my daughter Venus."

I tried to think of whom I knew there, but drew a blank.

"I would like to meet with you first if that's okay?" he said.

"Sure," I replied, "I will be back in Deerfield Beach on December 28th. Would 1pm be okay with you?"

"That is fine and thank you so much for returning my phone call."

I hung up the phone and smiled. 'What a pleasant man' I thought to myself. He did not sound at all like so many of the arrogant fathers or mothers that I had dealt with in the past, who were trying to raise their children to be professional tennis players. Actually, he was just the opposite. The fact that he had put my schedule before his and even thanked me for considering him impressed me. I felt as if this could be the start of a good working relationship.

I continued with my Kansas Christmas, and five days later I was back in Deerfield Beach, basking in the sunshine once again. I had a busy morning schedule on December 28th, and Jim Tierney, the Director of Tennis at Deerfield Beach Tennis Center, was teaching on the court next to me.

"Hey Jim," I hollered to him on one of our breaks, "do you mind if I use your office at 1pm today? I have a meeting with this guy named Richard Williams about coaching his daughters. Have you ever heard of the Williams girls?"

He said that he had and that he had heard that they were supposed to be pretty good. He then cancelled his lunch plans, because he wanted to listen in on the meeting. Besides being a good coach, Jim was a real tennis enthusiast. He knew more about the history of the game than anyone I knew, and he still thought Rod Laver was the greatest player of all time. No wonder he wanted to stay and listen in on my meeting. If it meant that the Williams sisters were going to work out at his tennis center, he was going to do whatever it took to help make that happen.

Around 1:15pm, I heard a car pull into the parking lot. Looking out the window, I saw a big man getting out of a 1980's style, red Cadillac. He was wearing a dirty white Reebok t-shirt and a pair of navy tennis shorts that were slightly torn on one side. He was a husky man, about six feet five inches tall, with large features. His hair was messy and he had about a three-day growth to his beard and mustache, showing his age with a touch of gray. His face looked hard and weathered, which gave him an intimidating quality. As he plodded towards the pro shop, I noticed that he was not wearing any shoes. His monstrous feet seemed relieved and thankful for not being bound in leather or canvas. This could not be the man I talked with, I thought to myself, as he came up the stairs and entered the shop. Jim was in the reception area, stringing a racquet, and I was in the back office, sitting at his desk. I came out of the office and introduced myself to Mr. Williams. He held out his hand to shake mine and as I put my hand in his, I watched it disappear. His hand seemed to engulf not only my hand, but also most of my forearm. I felt the strength and calluses of his hand as it rubbed against mine, and I was afraid he would crush my fingers. I knew right away that I would never want to have those hands mad at me! Then he asked if there was somewhere private we could talk. We went back into Jim's office and Mr. Williams closed the door behind him and sat down.

"I have to ask you that anything we say here today be held in the deepest of confidence, no one else can know," he began.

I agreed, and he proceeded to tell me about his daughters. They were currently working with a coach in Delray Beach, but they were not happy with the fact that he could not hit, nor did he have any hitters that could challenge them. He wanted me to come in and be the hitter during those practices in Delray and said that there would also be other practices at an alternate site, where just he and I would be doing the coaching. At the time, I was working with Tammy Whittington, a pro on the WTA tour, who was struggling in her singles ranking, but doing pretty well in doubles. I told Mr. Williams that I was busy with her, but that I did have approximately three days a week open. He said that would be a good start and wondered if the girls could come by the next day, in order to watch Tammy and I practice and then possibly hit afterwards. I said that would be fine.

So, the next day, while Tammy and I were hitting, the red Cadillac pulled into the parking lot next to our court. Mr. Williams got out first and then the girls. 'They look like skinny little toothpicks,' I thought to myself. The stories I had heard about their power must have been exaggerated. They were dressed in matching Reebok outfits, and they each carried two or three Yonex racquets under their arms. They all walked up beside the court and stood watching Tammy and I hit.

After a half hour, Tammy had to go, because she had a tournament early the next morning. As we left the court, Mr. Williams began talking to Tammy. I noticed she was blushing and thanking Mr. Williams for the comments he was making to her about how good he thought her game was. That was the first time I saw what a smooth talker he could be. As Tammy was excusing herself, I walked up to Mr. Williams and he told his daughters who I was, then he asked them to introduce themselves to me.

"Hi, I am Venus. It is nice to meet you."

Again, I noticed the politeness. What a welcome change. I was teaching about eight hours of junior tennis a week and only a few of my students had such good manners. Venus was very tall for her age and had a skeleton like frame, which she carried very gracefully. She had white cornrows of beads in her hair, which jingled as she moved her head around. She had a firm handshake and looked me straight in the eyes with an animated, piercing look. If not for her age, I would have felt intimidated or defensive. Serena introduced herself next.

"Hi, I am Serena." She was polite also, but her physique was smaller and more solid. She seemed to shy away quickly or maybe she was just stepping back into Venus's shadow where she felt more comfortable. She also had the beaded cornrow hairstyle, but hers was pulled back with rubber bands to keep them in place.

"Now you girls go hit. I have to talk with Mr. Rinesburg."

He mispronounced my name again, but this time it did not seem to annoy me. Both girls kissed their father and then started slapping the ball back and forth, as if they were in a third set of the U.S. Open finals. I stood and watched through my sunglasses as Mr. Williams spoke. The power I had heard about was nothing compared to the athletic movements of these girls. In one rally, Venus crossed the entire court with two panther-like bounds and ripped a two-handed backhand down-the-line for a winner. In another rally, Serena chased down a drop shot and then a lob, before hitting a swinging volley to win the point. The talent was raw, but it was pure. I could see why everyone who had seen them hit marveled at their abilities. I became an instant believer in their chances of making it on the professional level. As Mr. Williams continued to speak, I listened. He wanted me to come to Delray Beach the next day and hit with Venus on the clay courts at the academy. At that time, he wanted me to let him know how many days a week I could hit with her. He took my phone number and I took his.

"Let's go girls!" he hollered.

"Ok daddy," the girls replied in unison as they came running over. Neither of them looked tired or out of breath, even though they had been hitting non-stop for the last fifty minutes.

"Thank you for letting us watch you today," Venus, the spokes woman, said.

"Yeah, thank you," Serena added as they climbed into the red Cadillac and drove away.

As I drove home that evening, I played the whole day over and over in my mind. That is what I do with everything in my life. I analyze something over and over until I finally think I have it figured out, and then I analyze it all over again. That is the decision making process that got me from Kansas to Florida, and that is the process that had me convinced that this was a project I was ready to embrace. Oh sure, things in my life would have to change. The time and commitment involved meant I would have to rearrange and reprioritize everything and everyone around me. But after all, wasn't that the reason I got into coaching tennis in the first place, to be able to help mold and prepare a player for the pro circuit? That was my ultimate dream.

II

I arrived at the academy in Delray Beach at 1pm. Mr. Williams had told me that they started at that time every day because the girls were too busy with their home schooling before then. Imagine my surprise when I pulled up next to the court to see them practicing already. By the look of all the balls scattered around the court, it was obvious that they had been out there a while. I grabbed my racquets and hurried out to where I saw Mr. Williams sitting. He was eating some fast food take-out and had a couple of people sitting around him. Venus was on the court, hitting with two guys.

"Hi Mr. Williams, sorry I am late," I said, thinking that he would reassure me that 1pm was the time we had agreed on, and that Venus had just started early. Instead, he just went into the introductions of the people that were sitting around him. 'Clever' I thought. He had me on the defensive from the very first day. After the introductions, he wanted me to hit, so he asked one of the other guys to step off the court. I hustled out to the open spot on the court and, with no warm-up, began returning Venus's powerful strokes. Little did I know at the time, that this would be how I would start every practice; cold.

Two on one hitting sessions seemed to be the norm for the first couple of weeks. I was asked to hit as hard and consistent as I could, so Venus could groove in her strokes. Hitting consistently hard was my specialty. My reputation was that I did not miss often and that I would try to chase down every ball like a yellow Labrador Retriever playing ball with its master. I did not know the meaning of the word quit. Venus would try to blast a ball by me only to see it come back either just as hard or with some variety of spin. Some days I could see it frustrated her. She liked to see the ball go by me and I started to get a feel for that, as well as a feel for her strokes. By the third week, I knew where she was hitting every ball and which shots she liked and disliked.

One day after practice at the academy, Mr. Williams asked me to meet him at a car wash in the downtown area of Delray Beach. I followed him there, pulling into the bay next to the one he pulled into. I got out of my car and walked over. He was putting quarters in the machine, as if he was planning on washing his car. He turned on the sprayer and held it out, spraying the water against the side of his car.

"I hope you don't mind, but this is to drown out our voices in case someone is trying to listen," he said.

"What do you mean? Who?" I asked.

"Well Dave, everyone wants to know what my next move with Venus will be, even the FBI. They may have planted bugs on me or on my car. I cannot trust anyone at the academy and that is why I contacted you. On Monday, we are going to start having practice at Pompay Park either before or after the academy practice. Just you, Venus, and me if that is ok with you?"

"Oh sure," I said. "Just let me know where that is and..."

"Shush!" Mr. Williams blasted, as the water had stopped. He pumped in some more quarters and when the water came back on, he began to speak again.

"I am going to move Venus's game to stage two. Can you write down for me what you think about all her strokes and what she needs to change and meet me at Miami Subs at 11:13am tomorrow?"

I agreed just as the water turned off for a second time. Nothing more was said. He got in his car and pulled away. He seemed serious about someone trying to listen and had me wondering what I was getting myself into. I went back to Deerfield to get ready for my evening lessons. I told Jim what had happened that day and expressed my apprehension. He said it sounded exciting and that I had to hang in there and find out what stage two was all about. We both laughed.

The next day I arrived at Miami Subs at 10:45am. He was not going to catch me off guard this time. Around 11:30, an RV (or land yacht, as I liked to call them) came rolling into the parking lot. Mr. Williams was driving. I could not help but smile, watching him maneuver the RV through the small parking lot and come to a rest next to my tiny car. He motioned me to come around the side and enter. I climbed in. It seemed as big as my apartment, with three rooms, a bathroom, a TV, and VCR.

"Is this yours Mr. Williams?" I asked.

"Yeah, I just love driving this baby around. Peoples sure get out of my way. By the way, just call me Richard." He pulled out a video camera from under one of the seats. "Do you mind if I videotape this meeting to show Venus and Serena later?"

"Uh, sure," I said. I was caught off guard again. He was good at keeping the ball in his court. He wanted me to read to the camera what I had written down about Venus's game. I did not have to read it though, because I had already transposed it to my memory. I spoke to the camera and critiqued all of Venus's strokes, giving my opinion on what changes should take place over the next year or so. Then Richard asked me some personal questions, obviously to judge my character to see if he could trust me to be a good mentor, coach, and friend to his daughters. He finally shut the camera off after he had gathered all the information he needed. I felt like I had been on the stand in a murder trial and the opposing attorney was grilling my character. I guess I passed, because he then told me his plan - Stage Two. He told me that he was not happy with Venus's progress up till this point and that he had decided to coach Venus on his own. He needed me to do the hitting and to basically act as his assistant coach. Practices at the academy would be as usual, but there would be an additional practice at some other courts, as he had mentioned before.

"Venus is going to become a serve and volley player," he said. "She cannot learn this by doing drills that every junior academy kid in America is doing."

The next three months, I drove over to the academy in Delray, did the hitting drills of the day, not saying a word to anyone, and then met Richard, Venus, and sometimes Serena at public parks all over Palm Beach County to do entirely different drills and hitting exercises. Richard's main focus was to get Venus off the baseline, where she had started to get planted, and push her into the net in order to use her long frame to pick off balls and end points quickly. He was convinced that she could be the next Martina Navratilova at the net. This was not an easy thing for Venus, who had become very comfortable smacking powerful ground strokes from two feet behind the baseline. She would charge the net off a backhand and I would easily pass her. She would drive a forehand and I would lob her. If she came in on a short approach, I would hit it right at her. The drills that we did in those first three months resulted in Venus getting hit a lot. In one drill, Richard, while standing on the sidelines, would fire tennis balls at Venus from an old grocery bag, while I was hitting Venus approach shots. You should have seen the look on her face the first time he knocked a few beads out of her hair. Shaken, but not stirred, Venus would keep going at it. 'That girl is tough' I thought to myself. Two points later, she was coming in again, frustrated, but sticking to daddy's plan.

One day at the academy, Venus was coming to the net on everything. It was not the drill of the day and she was being instructed by the academy coach to stay back and wait. The power struggle between Richard and this coach had me feeling very uneasy, and the constant contradictions had Venus confused. She kept missing easy balls around mid-court that she should have been putting away, and after one mistake, Richard, obviously annoyed, walked out onto the court, grabbed the racquet out of Venus's hand and yelled at her to do it a certain way. Then, as he tried to demonstrate the shot, he swung the racquet back and hit Venus on the arm. She gabbed her arm in pain, and tears began to stream down her cheeks. I was shocked! I got a sinking feeling in my stomach as I stood on the other side, watching all of this unfold. Venus being yelled at and then hit. I saw a fear in her eyes that told me that this was not the first time something like this had happened. I wanted to jump over the net and help her, hold her, comfort her. I could not stand to see her be bullied. It was as if she were my sister, who was being picked on, and I wanted to defend her. Therefore, on the next break, when it was just she and I standing by the water cooler, I put my arm around her.

"Are you alright?" I asked.

She brushed my arm away, said she was fine, and walked back to her side of the net to resume hitting. She was tough and although she did not want to let me comfort her at that time, I got the feeling she appreciated the effort.

It was August in Florida, and that meant hot, humid days and nights.

I would easily go through three shirts in one hitting session, and in order to keep a dry grip on my racquet, I needed two wristbands, a towel, and an extra absorbent over-grip.

Richard always had a cast of characters around him at the academy practices. One day, while I was on court, I noticed him talking to someone and then occasionally pointing at me. After the session, I got in my car and headed to the public courts in Delray for another hour or two of practice. When I arrived, that same man was there with Richard. I went straight out to the court, as I usually did, to try and stay out of all the sideshows that went on daily. Richard and the man came out to the court as Venus began hitting serves.

"Dave, I want you to meet Mr. Jim Pierce," Richard said.

Wow! This was the guy that I had read about, who was banned from the women's tour for his offensive behavior during one of his daughter's matches at the French Open. 'What is Richard doing, associating with him?' I thought. He had always criticized other tennis fathers for screwing up their daughters, but he seemed to be commending Mr. Pierce. I shook his hand, and he said that he had watched me hit at the previous session.

"You're a great hitter. Do you ever miss? You must be making two thousand a week!"

I managed a chuckle because I appreciated the compliment, especially in front of both Venus and Richard. It must have clicked something in Richard, because after practice he told me he was going to start paying me more and on top of that, he was currently working on a deal with The Walt Disney Company and the Campbell Soup Company. I would be getting my own unlimited credit card from Disney, and Campbell was going to put me in a commercial with Venus. He went into details on the specifics, and I was on top of the world after that meeting. This was the kind of payoff that I liked for all my hard work. Venus was supposed to be the next superstar and these were just the type of deals I could expect, since I was her hitting coach. As it turned out, I was pretty naive. Practices continued as scheduled throughout the month. I did receive a little more money each week, but nothing more was said about the Disney or Campbell deals.

I was starting to incorporate some of my own ideas into each session, with Richard's approval. I was also working with a male player on the ATP tour at the time, George Bezecny. I began to show Venus the hitting drills that George and I did daily, explaining the strategy behind each one. George was a grinder, he hit heavy, deep balls that would rip the racquet out of your hand unless you were in the right position to field it. He was from the old school of tennis, where points were set up and the opponent was worked off the court before putting them away. Practicing with him made Venus's ball feel light and fluffy. Richard loved these drills, because every one of them consisted of live ball hitting or point drills, the kind of drills that made you think, while running you into the ground. Venus also liked these drills because as she got better at them, she got to hit balls past me and sometimes at me. Venus's backhand was the first stroke to really start showing exceptional qualities. She could rip it flat down-the-line with control or roll it crosscourt for a pretty good angle. She would run around balls in the middle of the court just to hit her backhand. So, when we did the 'isolate and alternate drill' to her backhand side, she ran me around like a chicken with its head cut off, which she loved. The 'isolate and alternate drill' is where one player hangs out in one corner of the court and alternates each shot side to side, while the other player retrieves those shots and drives the ball back into that corner, trying to isolate the opponent's weaknesses and break them down. Both players will work hard, but the player who is alternating, obviously has less running to do and if their footwork is good and their strokes controlled, then by the fourth hit they should have the other player so worked off the court that the last shot is an easy winner. If practice was sloppy or Venus was having a bad day, I would go to this drill. A smile would come across her face because she knew she would be making me run. It is the greatest feeling in the world for me as a coach to see a student really start to master something. Their joy is my joy, their success my success.

A typical practice session during this time would go something like this:

- 5-10 minutes - Stretch, a couple of laps around the court.
- 10 minutes - short court warm-up (both players stand at the service line and roll topspin into the front half of the court.)
- 15-20 minutes - crosscourt backhands.
- 15-20 minutes - crosscourt forehands
- 15-20 minutes - down-the-line backhands.

- 15-20 minutes - down-the-line forehands.
- 10 minutes - Venus isolates one side.
- 10 minutes - Venus isolates the other side.
- 10 minutes - Venus alternates from backhand side.
- 10 minutes - Venus alternates from forehand side.
- 10- 20 minutes - Serving and returning.

If any one stroke seemed to be struggling or breaking down, we would stay on it until Venus felt like she was getting some rhythm. Sometimes Richard would start a practice with one thing in mind, like slice backhands, and an entire practice would be dedicated to that particular stroke. This was a good move because Venus did not have all the shots yet. In fact, she really only had a flat to moderate topspin stroke off both sides. Forcing her to hit other shots kept her from becoming too one dimensional, too set in one style. Venus's forehand was the side that, at this time, was out of control. She could hit it hard and some days she could even keep it inside the court, but all in all, whenever I put pressure on her to that side, she would make an error. The problem was her grip. She had an extreme western forehand grip, which worked all right on high bouncing balls, but lacked control on anything else. So why did she have this grip? Well, when she was younger and picked up her first racquet off the ground, she probably picked it up with this grip and it felt comfortable to her. You see, if you lay your racquet flat on the ground and then pick it up and start hitting balls exactly how your hand is on the handle, you will be hitting in a western grip. There are a lot of players who use this grip on tour, but most are deemed as clay court specialists, because of the high bounce they get on these courts. Changing her grip was not the issue at this time. Venus was comfortable with it and she just needed to learn how to use it. Lucky for her, it just so happened that I had the same grip. Mine however, had been developed on the fast slick hard courts of the Midwest, so I had mastered the low bounce as well as the high bounce. Although my advice to Venus was to switch the grip, it would be a few years before she would agree to that, and since Venus was not going to switch grips, it was my job to show her the tricks to using the western grip effectively.

Practice on August 24th was a hot one and not just because of the weather. Richard was again battling with the academy coach's approach to Venus's game. She was at the net that day, working on volleys, when Richard stormed out onto the court to correct how she was hitting the shot. He stepped into my place where I was feeding in the balls. I stepped off towards the back fence, expecting something dramatic. He had a look of disgust and much like before, I had an uneasy, nauseous feeling in my gut. He grabbed a few balls from the basket, and with a racquet in his hand, walked up closer to the net, showing Venus how he wanted her to hit the ball. All of us watching thought that that was it. He apparently just wanted to show her the shot, and even Venus put her racquet down by her side to listen. However, when he finished, he fired the ball from his hand right at her. She was not ready for it, so it caught her square in the chest. She frowned a little, but did not cry. The rest of practice, I tried to hit her the perfect ball so she could execute the stroke properly and keep Richard on the sidelines. However, as I mentioned, things were boiling this particular day and Richard made at least four more court appearances. The rest of that week, practices at the academy were canceled for me and I just did the private sessions at Pompay Park. Something was amiss, but I did not know what.

On September 2nd, Venus and I played sets at the academy. Richard was not around and Venus had a sadness about her. She was very quiet and lacked any kind of enthusiasm. I beat her 6-0, 6-0 in about thirty minutes. I tried to get her to talk, asking her if everything was all right, but she would not answer. Then I asked if we were practicing at the same time tomorrow. She nodded her head, picked up her racquets and left. There was still an hour left of our practice session, and I was left standing on the court all alone.

The next day, I arrived at the academy to find everyone talking and scrambling around. I asked one of the other hitting coaches what was going on, and he told me that the Williams' had left the academy and were moving to Bollettieri's academy in Bradenton, on the west coast of Florida.

THE
HYPE

III

In late October my lessons at the Deerfield Tennis Center were increasing with the coming tourist season. I was no longer racing across town to the academy for a midday practice session with the girls or having secret meetings with Richard at car washes, and there were no more extra practice sessions at some secluded tennis court on the east coast. It seemed as if the Williams' were gone for good and the roller coaster ride, that had only just begun, was over.

It was a Friday when a mysterious van pulled into the tennis center parking lot. It was blue with big yellow lettering on the side that read 'Bollettieri'. Jim Tierney was working in my place that day. He said that the van just sat there in the parking lot for almost thirty minutes before anyone got out. Jim was surprised when the doors finally opened and Richard stepped out of the van with a basket of balls and a racquet. He had a girl with him, but it wasn't Venus or Serena. They walked out to one of the courts and hit balls. Jim called me on my cell phone and told me to come over to the tennis center right away. I was about an hour from the site and said I would get there as soon as possible. I still wanted an explanation from Richard, so I jumped in my car and did my best Jeff Gordon driving to get to the tennis center. I pulled into the tennis center forty minutes later, but I did not see a 'Bollettieri' van in the parking lot. When I entered the pro shop, Jim told me that Richard had left about ten minutes earlier.

"So did you talk to him?" I asked.

"I did and he asked about you, but didn't say much else. I asked him how it was going on the west coast and he seemed like he wasn't happy with it over there. You should call him."

I probably should have called him, but he was the one who had left me hanging and if they were looking to come back, I thought it was up to him to call me. I felt as though Richard had taken advantage of me.

Another month went by, and the van story was becoming old, when Richard showed up at the tennis center again. This time I was there, teaching a lesson, and he came over to my court to watch. I could not help but grin as I looked over at him. He was wearing a white Reebok

T-shirt that looked as though it had the remains of the day's meals smeared across the front, he had shaved his entire head to show its bumpy shape and he was smoking a little brown cigarette. When my lesson ended, he came over and gave me a hug. He started into a story about how my teaching reminded him of some famous coach that he grew up with in Louisiana. I was still a little upset with how he had left and was just about to tell him that, when he said exactly what I needed to hear.

"Dave, Venus and Serena miss you."

I didn't know what to say. I have always had a soft spot in my heart for the underdog, the meek, and the humble. Those poor little girls were trying their hardest to make it into the pros, and it wasn't their fault that their father had picked up and moved them. He had thought that they would have better opportunities in Bradenton, but had found that this was not the case.

Richard had been promising me a contract since before they had left, so when he said he wanted to have a meeting to discuss the details of my return, I decided that I wanted more than just his word. Therefore, I packed a tape recorder in my bag and went off to meet with him in the tennis center parking lot. I switched on the recorder, and sure enough, he told me what he was going to offer me, as well as his low opinion of the Delray and Bradenton academy coaches. During one of his stories, the tape recorder clicked off, making a loud noise, but he just continued with his story. When we were finished, I met with Jim at a restaurant across the street, where I played the tape to make sure it had captured everything. It did!

Venus was all smiles when we both stepped onto the court. Together again at the academy. This time, Richard was assuming the head coaching duties. I was still Venus's hitting coach, and now Serena was hitting everyday on an adjacent court. There were different people showing up everyday, talking to Richard about sponsorships and offering him all kinds of money and opportunities. Richard was always pulling Venus over to the side of the court to introduce someone new to her. It did not seem to bother her, and some days I even enjoyed the breaks.

Venus was a hot item to every major athletic brand on the market. The hype about how good Venus was going to be kept growing every week. The media did their job of building the hype by writing articles predicting Venus's rise to number one, and Richard kept it alive by keeping Venus out of junior tennis and preaching that her education would come first or she would never play a WTA event. This was a great strategy at the time because of all the drama the women's tour was going through with Jennifer Capriati being arrested for drugs, Mary Pierce's father being banned from the tour and other tragic stories of girls burning out because of turning pro at too young an age. The WTA was so concerned about another burnout story that they were considering passing a mandatory age limit rule, dictating at what age a girl could play professionally. In light of this, the WTA loved Richard's comments about education first and they supported him wholeheartedly.

Companies were trying hard to sign his "Cinderella of the ghetto" as Richard touted Venus; she was a potential multi-million dollar endorsement deal. But they would all have to wait, because Richard made it perfectly clear that without an education, Venus would not play professionally. This buzz of anticipation turned the courts into a three-ring circus. Some days, the media would be in the parking lot as I pulled up, and reporters would ask me for comments on how Venus was progressing. I would not give them anything, I knew better. The quickest way out of my current coaching duties would be to start shooting my mouth off to the media. Besides, I had learned to expect the unexpected with Richard, and if he thought for a second that I was giving information to the press, he would have to fire me in order to maintain his control of the situation. Anyway, he was doing enough talking for both of us. I would tell him that Venus's forehand was starting to become more powerful, and he would tell the media, "The thunder claps whenever Venus strikes her forehand!" A quote like that would spawn articles in every local newspaper and maybe even some national papers. He had them eating out of his hand, and Venus liked the attention. When she jumped off both feet and hit a winner off her forehand side she would holler over to Richard and say, "Did you see that daddy? I hit the thunder forehand!" Richard would hoop and holler back, and Venus would smile from ear to ear. Anyone watching would get caught up in the excitement and smile too, heck I would smile. It was a fun time because Venus and Serena were just little girls, and since education had become the scapegoat, there was not as much pressure on them to perform. Even if a practice session did not go well, it did not matter in the Williams' big picture.

One day at a practice session, I noticed a group of suits had come in and sat down in the bleachers with Richard. A 'suit' was our nickname for the corporate salesmen of some company. Suits came and went all the time, but for some reason these particular guys caught my eye. Even Venus asked me, during a water break, who I thought they were. I had a pretty good idea, since they were all wearing Nike tennis shoes. That is what caught my attention and I am sure Venus's too. As Venus and I continued practice, I kept an eye and an ear open to the bleachers. Nike was considered number one to most players looking for sponsorship. They were known for signing the top players by out-bidding everyone else in contention. Knowing Richard though, I was sure it was not Nike that was impressing him, but vice versa. I started kidding with Venus during one of our changeovers.

"So 'Air Venus', what do you want to do now?"

She smiled. Serena on the next court tried to take her breaks at the same time as Venus, so we would all end up by the water cooler and she could join in on the conversation of the day. Today the talk was all about Nike and Serena was excited because she knew that when the suits came by, it always meant free shoes and stuff to try out and Serena liked Nike.

"Do you think they have got our sizes Venus?" Serena asked.

"Of course they do," Venus answered with certainty. She had learned how the sponsorship game was played, while Serena was still a beginner in that area.

"What about my size?" I added, since I had not yet learned how to get free merchandise out of potential sponsors. They just looked at each other, laughed and rolled their eyes.

When practice was over and the girls had left, Richard called me over to meet a couple of the suits. They were really nice guys, and since Richard had introduced me as 'the guy with the golden strokes who never misses', I guess they felt obligated to give me the red carpet treatment, usually reserved for their prospective clients. I did not mind, as I was getting used to all the attention.

"I love those shoes with that suit," I told one of the guys, and he told me that it was how they dressed for all their meetings.

"We'll send you a pair," one of the men said, as they left the courts. I never did receive them.

I walked with Richard towards our cars, which were parked in the back lot. He told me all about the meeting and that Nike was offering Venus a twenty million dollar contract. I asked him if he was going to take it, expecting a quick yes answer, but he told me it was not enough. He wanted more than just money from whomever signed Venus, he wanted a company that would give Venus everything, including stock options, design control, a signature line, and support with inner city projects and charitable organizations. A company that would sign, not only her to a contract, but him as well. He was going for the home run of all home runs as far as sponsorships were concerned. Venus had not even played a pro match yet, but her stock was rising with every company Richard turned down. I thought this would be a good time to bring up the contract he had promised me weeks before in the parking lot at the Deerfield Tennis Center. He was feeling very confidant, almost cocky, since he had turned Nike away.

"So Richard, have you had time to talk with your lawyer about my contract?" I asked.

He gave me his word that he had, but then almost as if he knew I was not going to believe him, he said, "Why don't we write one out right now, until my lawyer can send you one."

He opened the trunk of his Cadillac and started digging through a pile of fast food wrappers, empty soda cans, and various car cleaning products, and then finally pulled out a single sheet of paper that had what looked like coffee stains on it. He began writing out the details of what I was to be paid, once Venus signed a professional contract. I was not sure if it was a legally binding contract, but it made me feel that I was a part of what was going on and that I was appreciated.

The next week it was Fila, then Adidas, and finally Reebok, all bidding for the chance to sponsor Venus. Agents from Advantage, IMG, and every major sports agency in the world were calling as well. Venus did not like being bothered by agents. They were pushy and always asking personal questions, searching for information they could use to sway Richard in their favor. If an agent came out on the court or tried to talk to Venus through the fence, Richard would go ballistic. He had a strict policy that no one was allowed near the girls during practice time, no pictures, and definitely no interviews!

One day, a friend of mine, Phil, was visiting me from Kansas. He had never been to South Florida before and was here mainly for the sun and the beaches, but he loved tennis and had taught and played for over twenty years. He had helped me with my serve and was happy to see that I was passing on some of that technique. He wanted to come by and watch some of my practice with Venus. I told him he should come around 3 o'clock because that would be towards the end of practice and I would be able to introduce him to the girls and Richard. As it turned out, Phil showed up early, and I was not looking for him because I was concentrating on the practice session. Instead, Richard was the one who spotted Phil while he was trying to snap a picture from some bushes behind our court. Richard got up and left the court, I did not think anything of it because he always came and went during practices. But this time he was walking fiercely over to where Phil was standing. He laid into him and eventually kicked him out of the tennis center. I did not see or hear any of the incident, but when I got to my car after practice Phil was there, a little nervous.

"I hope I didn't get you in trouble," he said.

"What do you mean?" I asked.

He proceeded to tell me how Richard had threatened to smash his camera and sue him for invasion of privacy.

"I did not say I was connected with you in any way." Phil said.

"Don't worry about it Phil," I said. "Richard is always doing that to the media or agents, and he probably just figured you were one of them. If anything comes up I will smooth it out. Don't worry."

The next day at practice, nothing was said of the incident, so Phil was off the hook. Venus was full of attitude that day. I had seen her like this once before when Reebok had come and outfitted the girls from head to toe in their latest garb. Venus and Serena would always make fun of the designs of some of the clothing and today Serena was being especially rough on the T-shirt she was wearing. She pulled four new ones from her tennis bag and was going to throw them in the trash.

"Hey, I'll take those," I said.

"They're mediums," Serena said.

"I don't care I will give them to my friend if they don't fit."

"Ok, they're all yours," she said.

I took the T-shirts and stuffed them in my tennis bag. It amazed me how the girls would go through product. I was the benefactor most of the time, so I did not complain. I always had family and friends that would enjoy a new shirt or tennis racquet. It seemed Reebok was winning the race to signing the girls because it was their clothing that the girls wore most. Richard had already secured free product, from Reebok, but had made it clear that they would have to bid for an endorsement contract like everyone else. Reebok was being very generous and even offered me a free product endorsement deal. I was just ending my relationship with Mizuno, so I signed on to the Reebok team. From then on, the practice courts were one big Reebok advertisement.

IV

On the west coast of Florida, in the town of Bradenton, a similar story was being hyped of a young Russian girl at the Bollettieri Academy. Her name was Anna Kournikova. Some months before, the Kournikova rumor had reached us here on the east coast, but that is all it was, a rumor from the tennis underground. There was talk of this tiny Russian dancer, who could slap a tennis ball with the authority of a soviet hockey player. She had the athletic genes too, because her father was a former Greco-Roman wrestling champion, who worked in the Physical Culture Ministry in Moscow. She had been sent to America to train full-time at the Bollettieri Academy specifically to become a tennis professional. The rumor became a reality when Kournikova came to Delray, where Venus trained, to play the Junior Sunshine Cup. I was practicing with Venus on one of the backcourts, away from the tournament, and the buzz of having these two super starlets on the same property was massive. The media had already tried to build a rivalry between the two girls, even though they had never played each other, or even met.

Venus was curious, although if you asked her, she would dismiss the question, almost turning up her nose at the idea. Richard had a theory that no one else mattered. If the girls played their game out on the court each time, there was no one who could beat them. He instilled this belief in both Venus and Serena and it showed any time someone asked them how they would handle another player in a match. Kournikova was taking the traditional route to the pros, playing junior tennis tournaments, and training at an academy - just the opposite of the Williams camp approach. Richard had decided, after Venus had won 63 matches in a row in the juniors 12-division in California, that enough was enough. Venus would train only for the pros and not play any more junior tournaments. This went against every tradition of the sport and the media began to criticize this move, citing how the lack of match experience would hurt Venus in the long run. What was Richard's reasoning?

Well, about this same time, another young player on the WTA was having some personal problems. Jennifer Capriati was projected to be the next heir to the Chris Evert throne of women's tennis. She had come onto the scene at age fourteen and won the hearts of everyone with her bubbly smile and happy bounce in her step. With Chris Evert and her rival Martina Navratilova retiring, the woman's game was suffering and searching for the next torchbearers to light the future. Capriati was supposed to be the answer. She was for a few years and then, for whatever reasons, Capriati suffered burnout and dropped the torch that was put on her to carry. She was arrested for marijuana possession and then tagged with a shoplifting citation when she walked out of a store without paying for a fifteen-dollar ring. This was Richard's defense to all the criticism the media was directing at him concerning Venus's lack of tournament matches. He said he was not going to raise his daughters to be a flash in the pan, a burnout or get an injury by the age of nineteen and he used other examples from the women's game, besides Capriati to support his case. Therefore, with the women's game in trouble, the WTA began its campaign on passing the age eligibility rule. This move by the WTA took the pressure off Richard to enter Venus into junior tournaments. The following are a few of Richard's rebuttals: "Any parent who lets their daughters turn pro at fourteen should be shot and rushed off to join the Russian army!", "My daughters aren't going to grow up hating me for ruining their childhood", and "There's too many parents trying to live through their children in the juniors. I'll never do that, I'm too busy with starting my businesses."

After Kournikova left Delray and returned to her side of Florida's training grounds, practices were a little quieter. Venus seemed more determined than ever and was working harder. I think she was a little jealous at all the attention Kournikova had gotten, while on her turf. I did not know until I read about it later, but Venus had snuck a peek at Kournikova while she was playing the tournament. A reporter had asked Kournikova if she had seen Venus practice while she was in Delray and she replied, "I saw her seeing me." Kournikova was self-confident and that made for answers that implied, 'don't waste my time, ask me something about me.'

So, Venus had been curious, but that is about all. She was definitely not intimidated and by no means worried that this little Russian girl, who was a foot smaller than her, was going to beat her to the number one spot in women's tennis. I was also curious and had watched one of Kournikova's matches. At that time, it was obvious to me that, although she had great hand and foot speed, an arsenal of angles, spins and drive shots, and a good mix of serves, she wouldn't be able to win a game off of Venus. In fact, a better match would have been Kournikova against Serena, with the edge still going to Serena. Venus's return of serve alone would have demolished Kournikova. Any serve without pace that came over the net, like a little bunny bouncing through a field of daisies, Venus would have vaporized with a jumping thunder forehand or a nuclear backhand. I know, because she did it to me and other hitting pros every day. You had to hit a heavy deep ball at Venus or she would just attack and move forward on you. So, as far as the Williams camp was concerned, the Kournikova hype was nothing to worry about and the focus was turned back towards the women already on the tour. Richard's argument of no junior tournaments was stronger than ever.

Serena was practicing more and more, as Venus was getting pulled away from the courts for one thing or another. Serena's ball striking was getting cleaner and she used her angles very well, but she clearly did not hit the ball as hard as Venus. I played sets with her for about a week while Venus was out with a sore knee. My ball was too heavy and deep for her to create anything, and she ended up hitting a lot of short balls in the middle of the court, that I would easily put past her. But every time I suggested we just stop and drill, she would get mad and say she could beat me easy. No lack of confidence there. It was almost as if she wanted to prove that she could beat Venus's hitting coach in order to get some of the attention that was being given to Venus. Don't get me wrong, there was not any animosity towards Venus, in fact it was obvious to me that Serena loved and even admired her older sister Venus. It was just that all the hype was to get Venus on tour and I am sure Serena was thinking, 'Hey I am turning pro soon too, don't forget!'

There were other junior players training hard at the academy in Delray and they also saw the attention that Venus was getting. Every week, those players, both boys and girls, would send challenges to Richard to play Venus. He would not allow it, but always offered to let them play Serena. He worded it to the coaches or parents of those players by saying, "Venus is busy training for the pros, but if your son or daughter can beat Serena, then I will consider it." Most only wanted a shot at Venus and would decline the offer, but occasionally, Serena would get to play another player. Richard would tell Serena to hit only to the players' strengths and do things that she was not accustomed to, like come into the net after every shot. Serena lost a few times because she was not a net rusher, but the strategy of only playing to a player's strengths was great, because it made Serena have to work her hardest to win. It prepared her for being on tour, where the players did not have definite weaknesses. One problem with this was that Serena did not like to lose to anyone, whether it was a male coach or another junior player. Serena wanted to win. I would be hitting with Venus on the next court, while Serena was playing a set with another coach, when all of the sudden I would hear, "You cheater, that ball was in. You cheater!" Serena would be hollering to the point of screaming at the coach to give her the point or she was not going to play anymore. If it continued, Richard would intervene and always give the point to the coach. He was trying to make her tougher by not giving in to her. He might stand and watch a little longer and call in balls out just to upset her more. Sometimes it worked, but other times Serena would get so upset that a racquet would go flying, seemingly no different than most competitive 12 year olds, but on a competitive level, both Serena and Venus were much older.

Whenever Richard sensed that practices were getting too intense or putting too much pressure on the girls, he would cancel a day, or even a week, and take the girls to Disney World. He was good at keeping it fun for them. He used to say that he believed it was family first, then education, then religion, and then maybe tennis. The bottom line was, Richard was going to be a parent first and his coaching and managing would all be second. I think that this is mostly what had me drawn to the whole situation. When I was growing up back in Kansas, I remember doing everything with my brothers, Rick and Tom, my sister, Charlotte, and, of course, my father and mother, Rick and Barbara, who were always there for us, guiding us. I love my family because of all those experiences we shared, and the William's family seemed to be on the same track. Venus and Serena just loved their father and they showed it by kissing him before, during, and after every practice. Whenever their older sisters were around, they were always hugging and laughing and just being happy. When their mother, Oracene, was at practice, the little girl inside both Serena and Venus would come out. During breaks, all I would hear is, "mommy"-this and "mommy"-that. It was very cute, and it reminded me every time that I was on court with little girls, not mature adults.

Venus was growing like a weed. She was about five foot eight inches tall when I first started with her and now at five foot eleven inches tall, she was about to overtake me. She could now stare me down eye-to-eye and every day we had to measure to see who was taller. Since she was getting close in height to me, and rubbing it in, I decided to play a little trick on her. It seemed Mondays were her favorite measuring day, so on those days I always wore an extra shoe liner that boosted me to six foot one inch. The next Monday at the measuring session, she thought something was up, as I seemed taller, but I convinced her that I must have been slouching last time, and then rubbed in the fact that she would always be shorter than me. That worked for a couple of weeks, but then one day I was late for practice and came out to the court with my shoes in my hands, as I had been changing in the car on my way over and had not put them on yet. I set my shoes down to put on another pair of socks and Venus spotted the inner liner. She grabbed the shoes and yanked out the extra pad.
"I knew it," she said.

I busted up laughing, and she threw water from the fountain on me, which started a huge water fight that included Serena. Once everything settled back down, she demanded we measure without shoes and sure enough, we were dead even. She pranced around like she had just won the lottery or something. After that, we never had to measure again, as Venus passed six foot.

Venus's game in early 1994 was beginning to come together. The notes I had taken to date on all her strokes at that point looked something like this:

Athletic ability - Has great hand-eye coordination, quick first step, great vertical jump and soft hands at the net. Covers the court in two or three leaps. Covers the net each way with one crossover step.

Forehand - She has great racquet head speed, which makes this stroke a potential weapon. Makes a lot of errors because she goes for everything on every shot. Needs to add variety to this stroke. Has trouble with the low ball short.

Two-handed backhand - Venus's best shot at this point. Takes the ball early and on the rise every time. Has great disguise and versatility. Crushes the backhand return as good as anyone on tour.

Volley - It isn't the strongest part of her game because of her lack of balance and strength. Her forehand volley is stronger than her backhand right now, but that will change as she comes to the net more. It's easy to pass her down the line.

Smash - She can hit this shot right handed or left. She loves to try and knock the air out of these shots. Her leaping ability makes it hard to get a ball over her head.

Serve - Like the smash, it is solid. Her height and good reach has her hitting around 100mph already. A definite weapon for her.

Strategy - Still plays pretty one dimensional, but is constantly working on new shots and new patterns. This will get better with time and experience.

Mental Toughness - Excellent. Hates to see a ball bounce twice. Doesn't get intimidated.

The entire month of January Venus and I played sets at every practice. At this point, she still could not win a set off me, but did start to win more games. She was getting better and becoming anxious to play a tournament. Richard was sticking to his original statement that she could not play until she graduated from high school. Serena was now playing sets everyday as well. She had a variety of hitting coaches she played against, and one day Richard asked me if I knew anyone that could play her and beat her bad. The next day, I brought my friend and tennis coach Dave Rempel, who is from Winnipeg, Canada. He had just gotten back from Germany, where he had taught for about a year. He had smooth strokes and a big serve, but did not like to move too much. His game was all about controlling the point from the first shot, either the serve or return. He could do just that with his serve and as far as his return, well, I have always jokingly told him that he had the second best return in South Florida, next to mine of course.

I introduced him to Richard and the girls, and then threw him into the fire. He was expecting an easy match, so I knew he was going to be surprised. Serena's return of serve was getting as good as Venus's, and sure enough, she broke Dave in the first game. He looked over at me on the changeover and raised his eyebrow as if to say, 'Rineberg what did you get me into?' I knew he still had not adjusted to the time difference, and I had told him it would be an easy match. He lost the next game and then won twelve straight. Serena made him work for it, but she still made too many errors at this time, going for everything on every shot. Richard thanked coach Rempel for coming out and told him that he would let me know when Dave should come out again. Both Venus and Serena also thanked Dave just like they had always done with me after every practice. They were all so polite and even Dave commented, as we drove away, on how refreshing it was to hear a thank you.

"What do you think?" I asked.

"Serena has some good angles and a good return of serve. However she's lacking the power that I noticed Venus had on your court," he said.

"Yeah, Venus rips."

V

One week later, I opened the morning paper to discover that the hype was back, and Venus had announced her pro debut to be in August. The tournament of choice was the Virginia Slims of Manhattan Beach,

California, which started August 8th. The family chose Manhattan Beach because it is only ten miles away from where Venus grew up, in the tough ghetto of Compton, California, where she can tell you stories of practicing amongst gunfire. The media was all over Richard, who had said earlier that Venus would not be allowed to turn pro until she was sixteen and a half, and that she would not be allowed to play if she did not keep her grades up. So just when I thought it would be two more years of hitting sessions, the moment the media had been waiting for was possibly now just six months away. Venus had some improving to do and it was not going to happen by just doing the same old drills over and over again. She needed to get match tough, but without playing tournaments how was that to be achieved? The next morning, I opened the paper to search the sports page for new articles on Venus. This had become a ritual of mine, since I seemed to find out most of my information from the media. Richard was very secretive about Venus's career moves, even with me. Sure enough, on the second page was talk of the pro debut. As I read the article, an idea came to mind. Richard was quoted in defense of not letting his daughters play junior tournaments and the article read: "If you're training for juniors, play juniors, but when you have to face Steffi Graf, you should be training for the pros."

"That's it!" I said to myself. I would become the pros, Steffi Graf, Arantxa Sanchez-Vicario, Martina Navratilova, and every other top ten player. I had always been very good at imitating the top male pros. During practices with George Bezecny, to lighten things up, I would play like McEnroe, Becker or my favorite, Connors. I had mastered every pro's moves, grunt, and service motion. George would crack up at how close I would resemble those players and how consistent I could hit, using someone else's strokes. So, instead of doing it for fun, I decided that in all the sets with Venus, I would play like a certain pro player for real. Venus could then simulate that she was on tour, playing girls in the top ten.

I had some homework to do before I brought this technique to the courts. I videotaped all the matches that were on TV during the next six weeks. I got seven of the top ten players on film and then proceeded to watch each one over and over again, putting to memory their favorite shots, service motions, and body language, including shot selection when they were winning and when they were losing. Then I would go to the courts and practice all the shots, trying to have the identical back swings, follow throughs, and ball tosses of Graf, Sanchez-Vicario, Martinez, Navratilova, Novotna, Sabatini and Fernandez. Graf was my favorite to imitate of the women players. An extra highball toss on the serve that would go out of camera view, if you had been watching on TV, and running around virtually everything to hit forehands. I then added in all slice backhands and not many volleys and voila, I was Steffi Graf. My next favorite was Conchita Martinez because of the way she leaned back on every shot to hit extreme topspin. Sanchez-Vicario was similar, but drove the ball a little more often and had no serve. Navratilova and Novotna were similar in that they were serve and volleyers, and Novotna's serve was similar to Becker's in how she rocked back and stuck out her backside. Sabatini had that distinctive walk, with her shoulders arched back, and the worst second serve of any top ten player. She hit the heavy topspin like Martinez, but also came into the net. Finally, Fernandez I had down pat because she was a flat ball hitter and had a two handed backhand like mine. It took about three weeks before I could change my game to one of theirs on request. The next trick was to introduce this idea into the practices with Richard's approval.

Richard liked to be in control of everything the girls did on and off the courts. He would not let a practice start without giving specific orders to the girls. Even if he was not there, it was obvious that the girls had been told what they should do in each practice. I was not the type of coach who had to be in control. If the girls practiced to preordained orders by their father, then that was fine by me. It did not bother me like it did some of the other coaches that had come, got frustrated, and then never showed up again. There were so many coaches and agents calling Richard to say that they were the ones to take the girls to the top of the game. I had learned that no one got on to the court with Venus or Serena that was not hand picked by Richard himself. I was right where I wanted to be, in a position to help a young girl's career and be a good mentor.

When we started playing sets again, I decided to just start playing like Graf for a while, since she was number one in the world at the time. I lost a few games trying to slice even when Venus charged the net. It was much easier for her to get my passing shots off my backhand side and she noticed that I was not passing her much on that side.

"How come you're slicing so much?" she asked.

I walked up to the net where she was standing. "I'm playing you like Graf would play you."

"Why?" she asked.

My answer was simple; "She's the best in the world right now, so if you can beat her, meaning me, then you can beat anyone."

Venus gave me a stare, with her head tilted towards one side and eyes narrowed, which meant that she heard me and that she would have to think about it for a while to see if what I had said fit into her view of the lesson. I won both sets 7-5, 6-2 and afterwards, could not resist a little nudging.

"Well, I guess you're not ready for the best. Next time I'll play you like number 3 or 4." I let out a little laugh to let her know I was just kidding, however, Venus did not even crack a smile. I guess she did not find it that funny.

We would still do drills in the first part of every practice session. Venus was working on becoming more consistent, but what she really loved to do was practice new shots. One day at practice, she hit a shot that just floored me. We were doing a crosscourt, down-the-line pattern drill, where either of us could approach the net on the other if a short ball was hit. I approached and ripped a forehand down-the-line to her backhand corner. I thought for sure that I had a clean winner, as Venus was on the opposite side of the court, but in two gazelle-like leaps she had changed direction and was tracking my shot. The ball was about to bounce for the second time and I thought she might be able to slice it back, because she was not close enough to the ball to hit her powerful two-handed backhand. I relaxed a little, awaiting a floater or a framer, when Venus switched her racquet to her left hand and ripped a topspin shot past me. I stood at the net a moment with an amazed look on my face, while Venus collected herself, as if the shot was no big deal.

"Wait a minute, what hand did you use there?" I asked.

"My left," she said with a big grin on her face.

"Let me see that again," I said and fed her a ball I had in my pocket.

She turned on it like any lefty would and ripped another one past me. Now I had to grin. This girl was so athletic it was not even funny. I tried to hit her a ball with my left hand to start the next rally and it was so weak that she just crushed it for a winner. Then she switched back to her left hand and the challenge was on. The rest of drill time was all done left handed, and she totally kicked my butt. I left practice that day, thinking that she would have no problem being ready for her debut, but would the debut be ready for her?

VI

The media hounds were bothering Venus again, so we switched some of our practice sessions to the Deerfield Tennis Center. There were two courts that were isolated from the rest of the tennis center and that was where Richard liked to practice. It was a hard court facility and Venus could not practice there all the time because of her knees. She was growing so fast, that her tendons in her knees were weak and got sore from all the pounding. Anyway, two days was usually enough to clear the local reporters away from the academy courts in Delray. I always liked it when we were at Deerfield because of the fact, that there were no off-court antics going on and practices were usually more focused. Of course, Richard's cell phone would ring about ten times every half hour and if he did not want to talk, he would give his standard answer that I had been hearing now for over a year, "I'm in a meeting right now, can you call me back later?" He would use that line even if we were sitting on the hood of his car talking about nothing. By being around him, I learned how much he loved to play the fool to people on the phone or misdirect them into believing whatever he wanted them to believe. I guess he was just trying to stay one step ahead of everyone.

One day, practice had been rained out just before starting. I had nowhere to go for a few hours, so I stayed around to talk with Richard about Venus's game. Well, instead of tennis, all he wanted to talk about were his latest deals. In between the cell phone calls, he told me how he and some investors from China had just bought one hundred miles of airspace over India, and that any time a plane or a helicopter flew through that zone they had to pay him a fee. Of course, I never believed that story, but my father had always taught me to respect my elders and to listen when they talked. So I listened to how he and these same investors had made a move to purchase Rockefeller Center in New York. Another great story, but was it true? I didn't care either way. I went home and wrote down the stories because I did not want to forget them. They had amused me and entertained me through the rain delay and after that, I carried a pen and notebook with me everywhere I went, in order to chronicle Richard's stories and all the craziness that surrounded Venus, Serena, and myself. When things seemed somewhat sane or the roller coaster ride seemed to be on level track, I could always count on Richard to create some sort of excitement.

Venus was relentless during our practices in early June. There were only two months until her debut tournament and she obviously did not want to lose. It was hot practicing in the summer sun of South Florida, and between 1pm and 3pm the heat index was at its peak.

"This will make you tough V," I said during a water break.

"Yeah, I know camel," she said with a smile.

"Camel?" I asked.

"Yeah, that's our new nick name for you," Serena said.

Apparently, Venus and Serena had nicknamed me 'the camel' because I never had anything to drink at practice. The courts where we practiced did not have a working fountain, and because I was always rushing across town to get to practice on time, I never had time to stop and pick up something to drink. So I did not drink on changeovers or breaks. The girls would go to their jugs of water or Gatorade, which they had brought from home, and I would just towel off or grab a sixty-second seat. And so it went, the hotter it got, the more the girls would tease me. Occasionally, they would offer me a drink of their water, but I did not want to take anything away from their practice. Besides, I kind of liked the tough guy image, which I had with the girls, and I also believe that it made them work harder on the hot days. They didn't complain as much knowing I was practicing just as hard as they were, and without water to boot.

One day, Venus and I were playing sets and the heat was unbearable, even for me. I had not brought any water as usual, and Venus offered me a drink. She poured me a lid full of her jug and I gulped down the clear cold liquid. When my taste buds caught up with the iced substance a refreshed look came across my face. I looked at Venus and she had that girlish grin as she could tell I was enjoying my drink.

"That's an unexpected surprise," I said.

"You thought it was water didn't you?" Venus chuckled.

"Yeah." But it wasn't, it was the new flavor of Gatorade called Ice. It was clear like water, but had a lemon taste. It was very refreshing and just what I needed. As I walked back out on the court I thought, 'what a good-hearted girl.' She did that because she knew I would enjoy it. She must have appreciated my effort out there every day. From that day on, Venus was not just one of the many players I coached. She was someone special, someone who, amongst the entire ego building hype, had remained good-hearted, and for me that meant more than any amount of money I was being paid.

It was August and the coming out party for Venus at Manhattan Beach was cancelled. Richard told everyone that she had not kept up her grades and until she improved her grade point average, she would not be allowed to play. The reporters, who had endured all of Richard's antics up to this point, were getting frustrated and wanted an answer as to when she would be allowed to play. The Bank of the West Classic was Richard's answer to the media. Venus had been hitting better, but her serve was still weak and predictable. I wanted her serve to improve before her debut, so we spent extra time each day working on a better wrist pronation, in order to bring about more power. Also, she had a hitch in her back swing that needed smoothing out. To get more wrist snap we used all Venus's old racquets that were broken, cracked, or just out-dated. I had her throw them high in the air, using the service motion. This feeling of throwing and releasing upward is exactly what she needed to generate a good wrist snap, which in turn gave her more power. To smooth out her back swing we worked on the timing of her toss in relation to the movement of her back foot. As with everything, Venus was a fast learner and was applying the changes in her sets by the end of the week.

One of the characteristics, that set Venus apart from other junior players her age, was her ability to make adjustments to her strokes or add new strokes with virtually no effort. If I said to Venus, "Ok, hit the ball down-the-line with topspin," she would do it. If I then asked her to hit the same shot with under spin she would do it. If she was unsure about how to hit a shot she would say, "show me." I would show her the shot and then she would just do it. It was like she had a built in computer that processed information and spit it back out through her racquet.

VII

While Venus continued her practices, another teenage phenom from Switzerland, Martina Hingis, had already joined the women's tour, and the top players were beginning to take notice of her skills. She, unlike Venus, had already proved herself in the junior grand slam events, becoming the youngest ever to win the 1993 French Open Juniors at age twelve. She turned pro at a $10,000 ITF/futures event in Switzerland in 1993, and was allowed to play two other tournaments in 1994 - both under $75,000. So, while the other phenoms (Hingis and Kournikova) were playing pro or junior tournaments, Venus continued to play against me and my imitations of the top players on the women's tour.

The WTA had finally decided that they would pass their age eligibility rule, limiting play for anyone under the age of sixteen. Venus, who had turned fourteen during that summer, would be grandfathered in and avoid the WTA's rule by competing at The Bank of the West Classic in October. This time there would be no excuses from Richard, because he knew that in order to avoid this rule he would have to let Venus play.

October came, and it was just one week before the tournament. I made some calls to find out which top players would be playing. Since Venus would go in unseeded, she would surely draw one of the top seeds early in the tournament. As it turned out, Arantxa Sanchez-Vicario was the first seed, so I planned a week of practice with Sanchez-Vicario's strokes in mind. Sanchez-Vicario was the hot player on tour at that time and was closing in on Steffi Graf as the current number one player. I showed up at the practice courts at our usual time of 1pm, but no one from the Williams family ever arrived. After an hour of waiting, I went into the academy office and asked one of the staff if they had seen or heard from the Williams'. Richard had done it again. He had called in and canceled practice, because he was taking the girls to a Jehovah Witness assembly, Bush Gardens, and then Six Flags in Atlanta - all one week before Venus's biggest moment in tennis. 'Expect the unexpected' was becoming my motto when working with Richard.

So, the tournament started, and all the hype over the last two years from Richard, the media, and various coaches and ex-professional players was about to be placed on the table for the whole world to judge. Without any practice the week before, I must say I feared that it could be disastrous. Venus was as confident as ever, even though she had not played a tournament in over three years. Before her first round match against Shawn Stafford, she told the media they could expect to see her serve and volley, play aggressively, and, over-all, play very well. She did just that, whipping the number 59th ranked Stafford 6-3, 6-4. I was very excited. Venus had gotten past the first round with a convincing win and now faced the top seeded Sanchez-Vicario in the second round. The media was in a frenzy. Some predicted a blow out by the top seed and others a straight set upset by Venus. The veteran Sanchez-Vicario was undoubtedly the overwhelming favorite in my book. She had already won the French Open and U.S. Open in 1994 and had been a finalist at the Australian Open. Most experts believed her to be the best player in the world at the time, even though Steffi Graf was still ranked ahead of her. Throughout the year though, in Venus's practice sets against my Sanchez-Vicario type hitting, she had done very well, stretching me a few times into tiebreakers and breaking serve quite easily by attacking, so at least she had a chance.

Venus overwhelmed Sanchez-Vicario early in the match, using her powerful ground game to attack the much smaller (5'6") Sanchez-Vicario, and win the first set 6-2. Venus continued to roll in the second set, stunning Sanchez-Vicario by jumping out to a 3-1 lead. Just three more games and Venus would rock the tennis universe with the most stupendous upset since an unknown fifteen year old named Chris Evert beat the great Margaret Court in 1970, right after Court had completed her historic grand slam. Sanchez-Vicario was a fighter though, and she knew how to change strategies to turn a match around. At 3-2 in the second set, she began to play more to Venus's forehand. Even though Venus was making more errors, she still had several opportunities to close out the second set, including a break point to go ahead 4-2. But Sanchez-Vicario was no quitter and rallied to win the second set 6-3. Venus made a valiant effort, but she finally ran out of gas in the third set, losing 2-6, 6-3, 6-0.

Venus had lived up to the hype and the tennis world had taken notice. No longer would there be questions of whether or not she could play against the top players, or whether or not she was too young. Now the only question that everyone wanted answered was when would Venus's next tournament be. Richard had entertained the media during Venus's match by rooting against her in the stands. He said it was because he did not want her to win since he was against her turning pro at her age in the first place. It made for good press, and was just the beginning of what I call the 'Richard Williams show' that would appear at tournaments around the globe in the future.

When Venus and Richard got back to Florida, numerous reporters met them at the airport. The hype was stronger than ever and when asked if Venus was to be the next number one player in the world, Richard's answer was:

"Have you seen my other daughter Serena play? She's better than Venus."

BUILDING
A
GAME

VIII

I grew up in a small town in Kansas where people don't buy into hype. If you don't put up, you shut up. Venus had put up, but she had also shown some of her weaknesses. For one, she was out of shape. Sanchez-Vicario had run Venus into the ground to win that match, and as a coach I believe that getting tired should never be a reason to lose. It just means you were unprepared going in. Every great fighter knows not to go into a fight unprepared. Tennis is a sport that is similar to hand-to-hand combat, and good preparation can be all that separates two players. Venus needed the mindset that every time she stepped onto the court, she was going in to fight a battle and if she was prepared, then she would win. I was very keen on fitness for all the players I had worked with throughout the years, and because of that, I had developed a fitness program specifically designed for tennis players. I call it the 'Futuremetrics' program, because it combines plyometrics and tennis specific movements with cutting edge training drills that enhance the senses of touch and sight. Venus one day asked me what I was doing to stay in such great shape. She said my endurance seemed infinite. She knew I was hitting with George Bezecny every day for two hours before I came to hit with her, and when I told her about 'Futuremetrics', she told her father. The next day, Richard asked me about 'Futuremetrics', and I explained to him that it was a tennis specific workout program that took about an hour each day. He then asked me to explain some of the program, so I showed him the following itinerary I had in my notebook:

- 10 minute warm up stretch
- 10 minutes of twenty-five yard knee ups (jog, pulling your knees up to your chest as high as you can)
- 10 minutes of twenty-five yard butt kicks (jog, kicking your heels up behind you, so they kick your butt)
- 10 minutes of twenty-five yard ankle kicks (jog, kicking your ankles out in front of you like the leader of a marching band)
- 10 minutes of twenty-five yard sprints
- 10 minutes of box jumps (jumping on and off a two feet high wooden box)
- Cool down stretch.

I explained to Richard, Venus, and Serena that I did this every morning at exactly 7am with some of the other players I coached, and that they were welcome to join. Richard said that they would be there bright and early the next morning.

I was at the park next to the Deerfield Tennis Center around 6:30 the next morning. One of my college players, Alan, was there with me, as he was working very hard on improving his quickness and stamina. I had told him the night before that Venus and Serena Williams might be joining our workout, and he was looking forward to meeting the two girls that the tennis world was talking about.

7am came and there was no sign of the Williams', so Alan and I began our workout.

"So, are you going to make them run suicides Coach?" Alan asked.

He said that because he knew the story of another one of my college players, Nick, who once showed up forty-five minutes late to practice and had to run forty-five one hundred yard sprints because of his tardiness. I was always on time, so I expected my players to be on time too. Alan was hoping to see me make these so-called phenoms burn for their tardiness.

"No," I said. "I can't be quite as tough on these girls. Besides, they are driving down from Palm Beach, which is over an hour away. I have to cut them a little slack."

"You're getting soft coach," Alan said. With that we went out to the baseball fields adjacent to the tennis courts and began our workout.

The Williams' red Cadillac pulled into the parking lot at 7:15am. Venus and Serena jumped out and hustled to the field where Alan and I were working out. I introduced everyone and proceeded to take the girls through each of the 'Futuremetrics' drills of the day. After about an hour, the girls were beat. They had done all the drills and shown great athleticism throughout each one, but they were gasping for air and parched for water by the end. I figured that they needed a 6 week/5 day program to really get in shape, and then probably a 3 day/week maintenance program. Richard liked what he saw and wrote down a lot of footwork drills we were doing for home use. I told him that this was just one day of the program, that the drills changed slightly each day and that he hadn't even seen the senses drills.

"Could you write out the senses drills for me, Dave?" Richard asked.

"I'll bring them to practice this afternoon," I answered.

The following are some of what I call my 'senses drills', as they are used to enhance the senses of the body and mind.

The Eye Patch Drill - cover one eye with an eye patch and hit balls into both corners from the forehand side, coach feeds fifty times. Repeat the drill to the backhand side for fifty hits. Then cover the other eye and repeat fifty hits from forehand and backhand sides. A player may discover here that one eye is more dominant than the other, or that both eyes are the same.

The Sparkler Drill - Tape a sparkler on the tip of your player's racquet. In the dark, light the sparkler and have the player shadow stroke a forehand, a backhand and a serve motion. Video record the laser light pattern the sparkler makes through the air. Show this to the player so they can have an exact visual image of what their patterns are on all their strokes.

Box Jump Drill - The player runs forward, jumps off a wooden box about two feet high, and then swings at a forehand or a backhand ball that is tossed in the air by the coach. Great for working on body balance in flight.

Strobe light hitting - Used at night with the court lights off. Place a strobe light on the net post facing into the court. Feed balls through the flashing light, having the player hitting all types of shots. Then turn the court lights on for fifteen minutes of normal lighting. The ball should be easier to track now that the light is not flashing and the eyes can see a constant ball stream rather than a broken ball stream.

Net Turnarounds - Have the player stand at the net with his/her back to the coach standing on the opposite baseline. Blow a whistle to signal the player to turn around as fast as possible to hit a forehand or backhand volley. The coach should change positions at the baseline as the players back is turned, so the player has to find the ball once he/she has turned to face the coaches feed.

I explained to Richard that these drills were used in conjunction with normal tennis workouts and not with the 'Futuremetrics' program in the morning. I wrote out a brief description of the drills on a few pages, which he took. I don't know if he ever used the senses drills because he never asked me about them again, but a lot always went on after I left the courts each day, so I would not be surprised if he showed both Venus and Serena at some point.

Besides being out of shape, the other problem that became apparent in Venus's match against Sanchez-Vicario was her forehand. She had made so many unforced errors off her forehand side that Sanchez Vicario had hit every key shot to that side in the second and third sets to take the advantage and eventually win. We started working on a more controlled ball flight, adding topspin to help keep down the errors off that forehand side. With Venus's western grip it was very easy for her to get more topspin. All she had to do was to pull up during her follow-through at a steeper angle, which would in turn allow the racquet to apply more spin. Venus could do this, but it just did not fit her personality. She liked to hit flat winners and rolling the ball back into play was just not her style. She spent about three weeks hitting only topspin and it was beginning to sink in. I happened to like practicing with Venus when she was hitting more topspin forehands, because then she was only able to hit winners against me off one side, her backhand. Before, in those practices when her forehand was on, Venus could slap winners off both sides, which meant that I had to run more and counter punch more than I liked to in our rallies. However, those days were few and far between and that is why Venus was working on hitting more topspin forehands. For those three weeks, my job was to hit 90% of my shots to her forehand, which meant long rallies and a lot less winners for her, but the extra topspin was teaching her to become more patient. In addition, her confidence was growing and it showed in her set scores. She had twice extended me to tiebreakers and even served for a few sets in that three-week span.

One day in early 1995, Venus and I were in a dogfight of a set. I was serving at 4-5 and playing a Steffi Graf style game, isolating Venus's forehand. She was not missing anything on her forehand side, and I decided to start mixing it up by serving more to her backhand. At 15-0 Venus took a good first serve to her backhand and ripped it down-the-line for a winner. At 15-15, I served wide to her forehand and she flattened it out and hit another winner down-the-line. At 15-30 I served and volleyed, only to get passed off her backhand side. At 15-40 I served into her body and won the point. At 30-40 I did the same thing to win the point and send it to deuce. Venus did not like to get jammed on the serve, because it did not allow her to take a full swing at the ball. Most players do not like the serve into the body, but it is especially tough on the taller, longer limbed players, like Venus, since they have to step further to the side in order to get out of the way of the ball. At deuce, Venus and I had about a twenty five-ball rally. I was mixing in some high loopers, trying to sucker her into going for a big winner. She remained patient and ended the point at the net by stepping into the court on one of my loopers and hitting a swinging volley for a winner.

Venus was showing all her athletic talent, and with another big return off her backhand, she had won the set 6-4. She went into a little celebration dance that included a few twirls. Venus had won her first set against me, and I can tell you she thought it was the bomb. We had spent an hour and twenty minutes on that set, so we did not have time to play anymore. There were a few more drills to do before practice ended and with Venus hitting so well, Richard wanted me to introduce some new shots. Venus spent the rest of practice hitting nothing but slice forehands and slice backhands.

IX

On May 22nd, Reebok announced that it had signed Venus to a five year, twelve-million-dollar endorsement deal. With only one pro tournament under her belt, Venus (or was it Richard) had hit a sponsorship home run. To celebrate the deal, Richard took the girls on vacation, so the next practice session was two weeks later. Richard commended me for all my hours of hitting and coaching and handed me the check that he had promised me once Venus signed a professional contract. I was shocked, but grateful, that Richard had kept his word on a contract that was written on the back of a piece of scrap paper from the trunk of his car. But what I remember most is that he was much more sincere and thankful back in those early years. His ego was still relatively small, though growing fast. People had not yet started asking him for favors or money. He was just good old Richard Williams, who seemed to love everyone around him, especially his two athletically gifted daughters, Venus and Serena.

The summer of 1995 saw many changes in the Williams' routine. First of all, they left the academy in Delray Beach and moved to a house in Palm Beach Gardens, some fifty miles away. Next, practice sessions were moved to a country club in West Palm Beach that was about forty minutes from where we had been practicing until then. Venus and Serena stopped their home schooling and enrolled into The Driftwood Academy, an accredited thirty student private high school in Lake Park, Florida. Richard was now handling all the head coaching responsibilities as well as managing and promoting. I was still hitting coach for Venus and Serena, but also hitting everyday was another very talented coach, Gerard. Gerard was a lefty, which was exactly what Richard was looking for at the time. Now Venus and Serena could practice returning serve against two types of players. The left-handed servers always have an advantage serving to the add court because of their ability to serve wide to a right-handers backhand. If you only play against right-handers, it is often difficult to adjust your timing when you face a lefty.

So everything had changed once again. I was used to change and it just meant that I would have to adjust my schedule once again to fit in with Venus and Serena's. Luckily their school was only half-day, so the practice time would stay between 1-3pm every day. The unlucky part was that I now had to clear an extra hour on each side of that time frame for driving, since the club we were practicing at was in West Palm Beach, about thirty miles north of Deerfield Beach.

The women's tennis game was going through some changes of it's own. Power was creeping in and pushing aside the long line of slow moon ballers who needed four to ten shots to win a point. The power players were now ending points with one to three shots per rally. The men's game had already gone through this phase in the 80's. More and more players were hitting outright winners from anywhere on the court. The art of setting up a point with a series of shots was gone. Now, big forehand and backhand combinations were all that was needed to leave an opponent dazed and confused. Combinations were a major part of my coaching. I always stopped to point out a good combination of shots by Venus and to explain to her why one shot helped set up another. Because Venus's return of serve was such a weapon, we worked on starting a combination straight from her return rather than waiting for a rally to begin.

Some of the combinations she uses today are as follows:

Down-the-line/Down-the-line - With down-the-line return, the response from an opponent is usually short crosscourt, which allows Venus to step into the court and rip down-the-line again. This is the most effective return for controlling the point.

Inside-out/Down-the-line - Venus uses this on any ball in the middle of the baseline, where she can step around the ball and hit an inside-out shot to the service line/sideline area. A crosscourt response allows for an easy winner down-the-line. Venus can hit this combination off either side.

Crosscourt angle/crosscourt deep - This was Serena's best combination because of her natural ability to hit great angles, but for Venus this combination took more practice than the others and that is because Venus was a flat ball hitter. Her balls usually landed around the baseline with very little room for error. This combination is started by rolling an angle ball to the service line/sideline area of the court and with a down-the-line or down-the-middle response, the next shot is hit crosscourt deep to the baseline/sideline area. As Venus's topspin improved, so did this combination.

One of the great things about both Venus and Serena was their creativity. I guess I was too structured in some of my thinking, which probably goes back to my childhood days when I just did exactly what a coach said, not even considering other options. Not Venus and Serena though, they could take a shot combination or a play pattern and make it work just as well in reverse, and they loved to prove that to me. Venus and Serena were still young girls and, although they always obeyed their father's orders, they seemed to like to joke around with me. Some days they would come to practice with their own agenda, and no matter what it was that I was trying to point out or teach, it seemed to just go in one ear and out the other. But that is part of coaching. Since you are dealing with personalities and emotions, as well as strokes and mechanics, you have to realize that some days your player is just not going to be receptive. A good coach has to be able to give and take.

The girls enjoyed their fun time at practices, and some days they were even mischievous. One of the antics they occasionally liked to pull at practice came to be known as 'opposite day'. If I was looking for a down-the-line/crosscourt combination to win a point, Venus would hit just the opposite and try to win the point. If I wanted Serena to hit a return and stay back, she would instead chip and charge, just the opposite. But 'opposite day' did not just apply to the tennis court. During water breaks, if I asked for the blue Gatorade, Serena would give me the red. If I asked to borrow a towel, Venus would hand me a hat or a racquet. I would just look at them with a puzzled face and they would burst out laughing. The first few times they did this to me, I did not understand, but as it happened again and again I figured it out. "Okay, it must be opposite day," I would say, and as long as I asked for the opposite of what I really wanted, the practice went without a hitch. Girls just want to have fun, right?

As I mentioned, whenever Richard felt the girls were getting burned out or over-practiced he would usually take them off the court, cancel practice for a few days, and go on vacation. But sometimes just a change of scenery or practice surface would do the trick. I remember the first time we hit on grass courts. Venus and Serena were falling down all over the place. Their speed actually hurt them, because there was no traction for their quick speed when they wanted to stop or change direction. Also, there were a lot of missed hits because of Venus and Serena's big looping strokes. The ball on a grass court does not bounce very high, so your timing has to be quicker and your positioning has to be lower. Venus quickly realized that she needed to shorten her back swings in order to help in the timing of a grass court bounce. We spent an entire week on the grass during the Wimbledon season of 1995. While all the tour stars were busy battling it out over in England, we were having our own pretend tournament right here in Florida. By the end of the week, Venus was serve and volleying and had compacted her strokes to fit the speed of the surface. She had the power already, and power is rewarded much more on the grass than it is on any other surface. I could tell that as soon as she learned to move around on the grass she would be unbeatable. At our last practice match, she confided in me, "Dave, I want to win Wimbledon. I like how the grass feels."

Back on May 9, 1995, Venus had requested and received wild card entries to three WTA tour events in August and October, so it was time to get off the grass and start practicing again on clay and hard court surfaces. The tournaments were the Acura Classic in Manhattan

Beach, California on August 7th, the Du Maurier Ltd. Open in Toronto on August 14th, and the Bank of the West Classic in Oakland, California the week of October 30th, where Venus had made her professional debut in 1994.

Venus had again been struggling with her serve. She still had a tendency to hitch or pause her back swing at the same time as she brought her back foot up. This caused awkward timing between her ball toss and her wrist snap. Venus spent extra time each day, trying to smooth out her back swing on the serve. One of the problems was that she was growing so much. It seemed like one month her timing would start to get better and then the next month, she would grow half an inch and throw it off. Then her knees would get sore so she would not bend as much and that would also throw off her timing. She was five feet nine inches tall when I started hitting with her. She was now six feet. That is a lot of growing in just two years, and her knees were consequently taking the punishment. In addition, her serve was struggling to keep up with her growth.

Venus went to California, while I stayed and practiced in Florida with Serena. In Venus's first tournament in almost a year, she lost to Sweden's Asa Carlsson, 6-4,6-1. She had played well the first set, but lost control of her serve and ground strokes in the second set, making numerous unforced errors. The next week in Toronto, Venus gave the then ranked 33rd, Sabine Applemans of Belgium, a scare before losing 6-4,7-6. She definitely overpowered Applemans the entire match, but again fell victim to herself, making over thirty unforced errors.

When Venus arrived home, it was obvious to me that she was glad to be back. She missed her dog, her mom, and she especially missed Serena. It was like the two of them were twins, and being separated not only upset Venus, but also Serena. Serena's practice sessions while Venus was away were unmotivated and stale. She cut practice short six times during that three-week period, claiming one injury or another. The truth was, she was slightly depressed and probably a little afraid that big sister was going to go off and become famous never to return again. But Venus did return and so did the spark in Serena's eyes.

Because of the two tournament first rounds in which she had played, Venus had a computer ranking for the first time. She was listed at number 313 compared to a previous month's ranking of UNC (unranked). I brought in an article showing this to give to Venus, but she already had ten copies for herself. She was glad to have a ranking, but very unsatisfied with the number. She was not going to be one of those players who hung around the top 200 for a few years, slowly working her way up to the top. No, Venus had one goal in mind and that was to be the number one player in the world, and she was not going to wait long to make that happen. In order to get to the top, you have to beat the top players, and for every player ranked above you that you beat, you get bonus points. Venus knew how the system worked, and she had taken step one in her quest by getting a ranking. She had one more tournament left in 1995 and that would be her last chance to move up on the computer.

Venus and Serena were not playing in the 1995 U.S. Open, but they would be watching, because this U.S. Open marked the grand slam comeback for Monica Seles, who had been out of the game since 1993. While playing a tournament in Hamburg, Germany, Seles was stabbed in the back by a psychotic fan named Gunther Parche during a change over. Seles was ranked number one at the time of the attack and was dominating women's tennis. Venus and Serena both admired Seles and her game of all or nothing shots off both sides. Serena could hit angles like Seles, but without the power. Venus had the power but lacked the angles. The finals pitted Seles against Steffi Graf. Just having Seles reach the finals was the comeback story of the year. Most did not expect her to give Graf much of a challenge, since Graf had dominated the tour ever since Seles's departure. But Monica had her own expectations, and she took Graf to three sets before losing 7-6, 0-6, 6-3.

Perseverance and competitiveness were the topics of my discussions with Venus and Serena during our next few practices after that U.S. Open. Monica Seles had shown great perseverance in just stepping back onto a tennis court after the stabbing. She had won her first tournament back, and reaching the finals of the U.S. Open was the best example of perseverance that I could give them at that time. Venus would like to have done better in her last two tournaments, and although her strokes were getting better and better, it would mean nothing unless she learned to make perseverance a habit. All great athletes must be willing to hang in there and keep trying no matter how great the adversity. "Seles could have quit the game. She had enough money, titles and fame," I told Venus. "But she didn't. She didn't because of something deep inside her competitive nature that said, I will not let this beat me." Venus understood, because she too had that quality. In practice sessions she would chase down every ball I hit. If there had been an electric fence between her and one of my shots, she would have run right through it to get that ball before it bounced twice. She hated to see a ball bounce twice. I would say, "that's perseverance!" All she needed to do now was to transfer that into her matches and her tournaments. I have found over the years that you can't teach a player to compete. Being a fierce competitor is something that has to come from within each player. I could help bring it out though, and I tried to bring up examples whenever possible.

In the 1980's when I was growing up and playing junior tennis, there was no player more fierce a competitor than Jimmy Connors. Connors only knew one thing - win at all costs. If it meant throwing his body through the air or running until his toes bled, then that is what he would do to win. A quote of his that I adopted throughout my playing career was: "I hate to lose more than I like to win." He would show that attitude time and time again in his historic 'come from behind' victories. Tennis fans had come to forgive him for overpowering and embarrassing their aging idols in the seventies and for his sometimes crude behavior on the court throughout the 1980's and 1990's. Who could ever forget his run at the U.S. Open title in 1991, where he had two five-set victories? During one of these matches, Connors got a questionable call against his opponent Patrick McEnroe. He was so upset that he stormed the umpire's chair like a Kansas tornado, screaming, "Turn that damn Cyclops machine off. It is worthless and so are you!" During his match against Aaron Krickstein, he stormed the chair umpire again and this time he shouted, "You are an abortion!" Despite his behavior on the court, tennis fans could not overlook the amount of heart Connors put into every point. Fans either loved him or loved to hate him, but they all loved to watch him compete.

Venus and Serena both loved to compete in practice sessions, but if things were not going their way, they had a bad tendency to quit or make up some excuse or injury explaining why they were losing. This was a dangerous habit being spawned because it took away their possibilities to persevere in the future. I would challenge Venus to comeback and win a set when she was trailing, but she was still too young to care. Let's face it, at this point she had not lost very often, except in practice, and everyone around her was telling her how great she was or would be, so why should she care. All I could do is tell her my Jimmy Connors stories and try to lead by example in our practice matches. Many times I would let her get a lead only to comeback and win. The rest would have to come from the still evolving competitor within.

Venus's last tournament of 1995 was The Bank of the West Classic in Oakland. At that tournament everything came together for her. She had been working hard on her new game, and she showed great perseverance and competitiveness to come from a set down, to beat 18th ranked Amy Frazier in the second round 4-6, 6-3, 6-3. That win put her in her first WTA quarterfinal event.

Back in Deerfield Beach, coach Dave Rempel and I were practicing at the tennis club when I got word of the big win. Everyone at the tennis center was so excited because of my involvement with Venus. They too had all become fans. Venus's next match was against Magdalena Maleeva, whom I felt Venus had a great chance of beating. But Venus got off to a shaky start and never recovered, falling back into her error filled game from before. Maleeva was the eventual champion, but Venus had picked up valuable ranking points, so the tournament (which was only Venus's fourth) was a small success, and it ended the year on a high note for everyone involved.

X

"The new tennis courts at our house are done Dave. Please meet us here at 1pm on Monday," was the message I got in the beginning of 1996.

I had not seen any of the Williams family in over three weeks. I had taken my usual trip home to Kansas for Christmas, while the girls had practiced for a week at an academy in Boca Raton and for a few days at the Bollettieri Academy in Bradenton. Venus and Serena spent that time beating up on the talented junior boy players and coaches at both academies.

I did not even know they were building tennis courts at their house, and I also did not know where their new house was located. Monday morning, I called Richard and got directions, but I ended up on a dirt road in the middle of a swampy tree filled part of Palm Beach County. I called Richard again to make sure I was heading in the right direction. Richard assured me that I was, and that I should keep going down the dirt road until it dead-ended. Their house would be the only one at the end of that road. The heavy rains from the night before had washed out and flooded much of the dirt road I was on. My car, a red Alfa Romeo two-seater convertible, had never seen a dirt road nor had it gone through water as high as its doors. I was afraid that my little car was going to stall out, and that I would be stranded in the middle of nowhere on one of Richard's wild goose chases. Although it took me an extra twenty minutes to get down that road, I finally arrived at a large plantation style, two-story white house with a lake and three tennis courts (two clay and one hard). There were several cars parked in front of the house and two abandoned cars out in a field on the north side. In the back of the house there were two barns and a dog kennel, which housed additional cars and various other items. The house sat on about ten acres, with miles of national wildlife reserve behind it and open acreage on both sides. To get to the tennis courts I had to walk across a flooded field, past one of the junk cars, past the dog kennel, and finally around a barn. There were no worries about privacy, which I am sure was Richard's reason for the move. Even if reporters or agents had wanted to find them, I would give them a twenty percent chance at best.

Richard informed me that practices would now be at the house in the woods, which once again meant additional driving for me. It would now take me fifty-five minutes at high speeds to make it to and from the Deerfield/Boca line. Once again, the sacrifices would have to be made on my end. The driving I could do without, but I did like the location. It was like an area I had grown up in outside of Towanda, Kansas, where I had spent my pre-teen and teenage years exploring the open range like a modern day Lewis and Clark.

Venus and Serena liked practicing in their own back yard. They had all the comforts of home, such as plenty of water and Gatorade, snacks, their dogs and anything else they were into at the time. Not to mention if it started raining, they could just race inside to the comfort of their own rooms. They had a jet ski in the lake, which was about fifty yards from the courts, which they could go ride around on if it was too hot out for them and there was now a small refrigerator between the courts that housed all their flavored drinks and bottled water. Our practices had definitely increased in comforts and I think that made it easier for Venus and Serena to concentrate on their games.

Venus's knee was bothering her one day, and so I moved over to Serena's court to do two-on-one drills with coach Dave Rempel, whom I had brought out to hit for the week. It did not take long before Serena suddenly had an injury as well. Venus and Serena were getting pretty good at faking injuries when they did not want to practice. Richard was out on his new riding lawn mower, which he had purchased a week earlier, and he did not seem to care. Since his new purchase, his daily ritual seemed to be to greet me as I came to the courts, instruct the girls on what he wanted them to work on and then hop on his mower and cut the ten acres. He would pull up to the courts every so often and make a cell-phone call or holler encouragements to the girls. When Serena left the court, he pulled over to chat with Rempel and I. He lit up one of his thin brown cigarettes, which he would smoke continuously, discarding the butts onto the courts. The edges of the courts had an ample supply of butts scattered just outside the court sweeper's reach. I could tell that it was story time, as he was getting himself comfortable on the mower seat and he had that look in his eyes that told me he had something to say.

"How was your weekend?" I asked him before he had a chance to speak.
"That's just what I was going to tell you about," he answered.
Just then his cell phone rang. It was someone from the WTA wanting to know if Venus had decided on her schedule for '96. Venus was turning sixteen this year and she was allowed to play a fuller schedule under the WTA rules. Richard gave his standard answer when he didn't want to talk.
"I'm in a meeting right now. Can I call you back?"
It reminded me of the numerous times he said that he was going to call me back and didn't. On rainy days, I would call to see if we were rained out and he would say he would have to call me back. Eventually, I would have to start driving to get to the courts on time and then I

would arrive and find out that practice was rained out. I learned to always call him back every half hour if necessary. Richard hung up the phone. His conversation with the WTA had him thinking and he had forgotten the story he had dreamed up for us, probably while he rode around on his lawn mower.

Then he said, "Dave, will you go inside and tell Venus I need her tournament schedule for this year, and tell her to make a copy for you too?"

I went inside to find both Venus and Serena in the kitchen eating pizza. I told Venus about the call from the WTA and she said that she had her tournament schedule upstairs in her room. As she went to get the paperwork in her room, Richard came into the kitchen and sat down at the table with Serena and I. Venus brought the tournament list and handed it to Richard.

"Daddy, these are the tournaments I want to play." Richard looked over the list and, grabbing a pen off the table, began to scratch out a few of Venus's choices. He left eleven tournaments, including Wimbledon and the U.S. Open. He handed the paper back to Venus and then scrolled down his phone looking for the WTA's phone number.

"You need to call the WTA and give them your schedule today," he told Venus, handing her his phone.

"And make a copy for Dave."

I sat there watching and again thought about how Richard was in control of everything. Nothing was done with the girls' careers that didn't go through him first, practices, interviews, tournaments, everything. Did he have a grand plan or was he just a control freak whose ego had taken over? There were a lot of people sucking up to him and letting him have his way, that was for sure.

Venus brought out a copy of the revised 1996 tournament schedule for me. The tournaments were:

- March 10th - State Farm Evert Cup
- March 17th - Lipton Championships
- April 17th - Bausch and Lomb
- May 5th - Italian Open
- June 23rd - Wimbledon

- July 21st - Bank of the West
- August 4th - Acura Classic
- ¤ August 25th - US Open
- October 6th - Porsche Indoor
- October 13th - European Indoor

This was a serious schedule and I got a rush of adrenaline while looking it over, realizing that my player (Venus) was going to be playing in all these tournaments. Wimbledon and the US Open stood out the most to me, since these were the two tournaments I had played over and over in my head against the garage door as a young boy. Richard took the schedule and with his pen he made a star next to three of the tournaments and then handed it back to me.

"We would like you to be available for these tournaments," he said.

My jaw dropped as I looked at the stars next to The Lipton Championships in Key Biscayne, the Bausch and Lomb in Amelia Island and the U.S. Open in New York. I had seen all these tournaments on TV, but now I would be traveling to them as Venus's coach. On the outside, I was calm and cool as I said,

"Oh sure, those tournaments will be no problem for me." On the inside, I was jumping for joy. I was not going to make any early arrangements though, as I knew that schedules were subject to change with Richard in control.

XI

When word got out to the media of Venus's proposed schedule, Richard's phone started ringing again. I showed up to practice that Friday to find a photo shoot in progress for the Men's Journal magazine. I stuck around because they wanted pictures of me with Venus. One of the reporters said, "let's get a picture of Venus with her coach."

Well, Richard didn't like that, and before he could get all bent out of shape, I quickly corrected the reporter and told him that I was the hitting coach and Richard was the head coach. Since Richard could not hit balls and I was the one doing all the drills on court it was easy to understand why people, outside of the tennis world, would just assume that I was the only coach. The truth is, that most successful players on tour have more than one coach. There is usually a hitting coach, a strength coach, and a conditioning coach on a player's staff. Sometimes there is even a mental toughness coach or even a diet/health coach. In today's game you need an edge any way you can get it, and if you have the resources there are a wealth of specialists waiting to assist you.

So, I did my photo with Venus and an interview with the reporter from the Men's Journal. He said that they were going to run the article and pictures in Germany first, where Venus was big news. It made sense; the Germans are some of the biggest tennis fans in the world. The whole country is so nuts about tennis that they have leagues set up there, where pro players are paid large amounts of money just to play in one or two months of matches. George Bezecny would make the trek to Germany every summer for a few months, because at that time he could make more money there than in the states. The clubs were allowed one foreign player on their teams and they all wanted the highest ranked world-class players they could get. Bezecny still held a high world ranking at the time and that was his invitation. The clubs were so competitive that they would pay a top pro like Boris Becker or Anka Huber a huge appearance fee for just one match that might give their club bragging rights over all the other clubs in Germany. Richard said that Venus was bigger in China and that the magazine should launch the article there first. He loved to talk about China and how popular Venus was there. One day he told me that the Chinese were offering Venus one million dollars to come over and play against Kimiko Date, who was their number one player. He told them that Serena would come for a million, but it would cost them two million for Venus.

"They're considering my offer," he told me.

The next week it was a Reebok photo shoot on Monday and Tuesday and a People Magazine shoot on Wednesday that disrupted practice. March was quickly approaching, and if Venus was going to play the Evert Cup at Indian Wells, she still had some game to work on.

Her first serve was too predictable and her second serve had too much spin and no kick, so it just sat up for an opponent to crush. Once again, Venus was being pulled in every direction and it was her game that was suffering.

I talked with Richard about my concerns that Venus was not practicing hard enough. I thought if she was going to play in two weeks that we should maybe do two-a-day practices, one morning and one afternoon. He disagreed and informed me that he had decided not to let her play the Evert Cup tournament because her grades were down in school. He was in fact going to pull her off the court completely for a week or two until she got her grades back up to par. He did pull her off the court, but then let her accept a wildcard into the qualifying at the Evert Cup. The result was that Venus had not been practicing and was going to play a tournament. Richard did things his way, and his way certainly differed from the norm.

Venus went to Indian Wells and won both qualifying matches, putting her into the main draw. She had a limited number of wildcards to use for main draws, so by qualifying she had saved one to use at a later time. She would now play Julie Halard-Decugis. The lack of practice had shown in her first qualifying match, as her timing was off on both her serve and ground strokes. Her second match was better and she showed good power on her serve. Winning matches was good for Venus's confidence and she went into her match against Halard-Decugis with no fear. But the veteran player was not going to be intimidated by Venus's power, and she quickly dismissed her in straight sets 6-3, 6-4.

I had been practicing with Serena while Venus was away at Indian Wells. Serena's game was improving, and she was starting to get stronger in both her arms and legs. The one thing that we worked on that week was Serena's crosscourt forehand. She had good angle on the ball, but she rolled it too much and it was easy to track down. If she was going to use angles as weapons, she would have to flatten them out, much like Seles does, so the shot becomes a winner rather than just a movement shot. Serena was getting especially good at hitting that shot off a wide serve to the deuce court.

When Venus returned to the courts for practice, she had stories for Serena and I about the tournament. The tournament, although not as big as a grand slam, is similar in that the men and women are both competing there at the same time. Venus had a chance to go see Pete Sampras play. She and Serena had this thing about Sampras; they just thought he was the 'Ultimate Player'.

She told Serena, "I got to go see Pete!"

"No way!" Serena answered.

"Did you fall asleep?" I interjected. "Don't get me wrong, Pete is a great champion. It's just that I grew up watching Connors throw his guts all over the court to win and Pete was just never like that, winning his matches with less effort."

Venus and Serena both glared at me for my comment and then continued their conversation.

"I want to serve like Pete," Venus said. "He gets so many free points!"

"Yeah, he must practice pretty hard on his serve," I said facetiously to get a rise out of Venus.

She glared at me again, and then said, "Let's go." She pulled the basket of balls back to the baseline and she and Serena began to hit serves. We stayed there until Venus and Serena could hit three different types of serves to all the corners of the service boxes. They would have stayed there all day and night if that would have given them a serve like Pete's, but everything was done in small increments, as Richard did not want his girls to injure themselves.

By the time April rolled around, Venus had developed some awesome power on her first serve. Although I did not have a radar gun, it was obvious to me that she was getting into the 100's just about every time. Richard pulled the plug on the Lipton Championship, but was happy enough with the way Venus was practicing to let her play the Bausch and Lomb championships in Amelia Island, Florida. This was one of the tournaments that I was requested to attend, and I was as excited as Venus was about going. She would again be playing qualifying first, so as not to use up a main draw wildcard. The qualifying was on Saturday and Sunday, and I had to drive up on Friday so I would be there to help her practice and warm up. I made the trek up I-95 and arrived at Amelia Island around 9pm. This was the time I was supposed to meet Richard at a Holiday Inn, to discuss practice times and procedures. I waited until 10pm in the lobby of the hotel, but there was no sign of the Williams', and Richard was not answering his phone. I went to my room and went to sleep, wondering what was going on.

The next morning I drove out to the tournament site to see if any of the Williams' had checked in or been seen. No one seemed to know anything. Finally, about an hour and a half later, I found someone with an answer. One of the tournament officials told me that Gabriela Sabatini, the top seed, had pulled out of the tournament with an injury and they had filled her place in the main draw with Venus. She would not be playing until Monday or Tuesday. I went to my car and drove the five hours back to Palm Beach. I tried several times on my way back to call Richard, but he wasn't answering. So when I got back, I went straight to the Williams house and knocked on the door. Richard answered, and was immediately all-apologetic for not calling me and gave the excuse that his phone wasn't working. He invited me in. Venus and Serena were in the living room watching tapes of old Monica Seles matches, and I could tell by the embarrassment on their faces that they knew I had driven all the way up to Amelia Island and that their father hadn't bothered to tell me about the schedule change. It was one thing to not call me when practices were canceled and have me drive an hour up and back, but a ten-hour round-trip was down right rude. I was about to disclose my anger to Richard when Venus asked me, "Can you hit tomorrow. I want to work on my serve some more?"

If Richard would have asked me I probably would have said no, but it was Venus doing the asking and I just could not say no to her. Maybe she sensed my pain and this was her way of making everything better.

So, Sunday we practiced. Nothing much, just some serves, returns and some forehands. Venus's hip was bothering her and Richard would have pulled her out of the tournament if Venus had not begged him to let her play. The call came in around noon from the tournament, saying that Venus's was the third match on after 10am, which meant that she would play around 2pm unless unforeseen withdrawals or injuries shortened the previous matches. The Williams' were driving up immediately to avoid any mishaps trying to drive up on Monday. I decided to wait. I could leave at 9am Monday and still make it to the tournament in time to warm Venus up before her match and then stay the night if she won. On Monday, I drove back to Amelia Island and arrived at around 1pm. I found the Williams' and Venus and went to grab a practice court to warm-up. The tournament was ahead of schedule and an official came over to inform Venus that she was next on Stadium Court. After a warm-up, Venus went to change and I went out to watch the rest of the match on the stadium court, so I could tell Venus when to start her pre-match routine. The match on the court had a veteran player, Kathy Rinaldi, playing in one of her first singles matches since she had returned to the tour after having a baby. Rinaldi was once a child prodigy herself and had lived up to her hype by becoming ranked as high as number six in the world in 1986/87. I watched her match and saw how she outsmarted and outworked her younger opponent by mixing in moon balls with drop volleys and deep ground strokes.

Venus came out, warmed up, and played six games. In the seventh game, she hit a first serve of 108 mph; the ninth fastest on tour that year. In that same service game though, she pulled up, grabbing her hip after a long rally. Richard noticed it immediately. He left the stands and proceeded down to the court, where he began talking to an official. Venus lost that game and went to her seat during the changeover. Richard came out on the court, and the next thing I knew, the match was over and Venus was going in to see the trainer. She had only been on court about twenty minutes, and after another ten minutes with the trainer, Venus was in the car and on her way home. I felt bad for Venus because I knew how much she wanted to play. She was not faking an injury, that was for sure. But Richard was overly cautious about his little girl and he was in no rush to have her on the tour until her mind and body were strong and ready. I was in no hurry to get back in my car to make the long drive back to Palm Beach, so I decided to stay at the tournament for a few hours and scout some of the players Venus might be playing in the future. While I was watching a girl from Romania, Irina Spirlea, I ran into a coach I had worked with back in 1990. As we talked, he asked me if I knew that Kathy Rinaldi was looking for a coach. I said I did not know, but I was too busy with the Williams sisters to take on another player. He said that was too bad because she lived in my area and thought that I would be perfect for the job.

As I drove back to Palm Beach, I spent the five hours going over my weekly and monthly schedules in my head. I concluded that with the summer approaching, things would be considerably slower at the clubs I worked, and if Venus traveled more, it would free up more of my time. Rinaldi would have to be flexible and work around my time with Venus and Serena, but if she was willing to do that, maybe I could take on another player.

When I got back, I wrote up a proposal letter to send to Rinaldi, but I did not mail it. I thought I had better check my source's information first. George Bezecny still had a beat on what was happening on the tour. As we worked out that next day, I asked him if he knew anything about Rinaldi. He immediately said that he had heard that she was looking for a coach. A friend of his had coached her when she lived in Las Vegas, Nevada and now she had moved back here and was looking.

"Hey, you'd be perfect for her," he said. That was twice someone had said I would be perfect for the job.

Venus and Serena were off the court for two weeks because of injuries and schoolwork. I used that time to get together with Rinaldi and set up a practice. We hit it off right away. I was hitting strong because of my work with Venus and Serena and that is exactly what Rinaldi needed, a good hard hitter who could push her around the court, portraying the powerful players in today's game. After a few sessions, we made it official, and I began coaching Rinaldi along with Venus and Serena. In the June issue of Tennis Week, the news went public. I wondered what Richard's reaction was going to be when he read the release: "Kathy Rinaldi-Stunkel, who left the tour briefly in 1993 and was formerly ranked as high as no. 7 in the world in May 1986 and January 1987, is making her comeback on the Corel WTA Tour. She has hired Dave Rineberg to be her coach. Rineberg has worked with several tour players and is currently the hitting coach for Venus and Serena Williams."

I do not know how Richard felt, but I was ecstatic. My friend Kevin Lewis, who was a tennis pro in Texas, had always said that Tennis Week was the bible as far as tennis magazines went. 'You know you've made it big when you get your name in Tennis Week,' he used to say. That is how I felt. I picked up every available copy to mail back home to all my family in Kansas. Venus and Serena always had copies at the courts, as they tracked Venus's ranking and results. Serena was the one who saw it first and she saved her issue for me to keep, which was a nice gesture on her part and uncharacteristic of her at the time. I think that my rating went up in the eyes of Venus and Serena. Seeing that a former top ten player of the tour was now working with me made my coaching comments to them more trustworthy and more reputable, I suppose.

XII

My schedule could now have me hitting for two hours in the mornings with Rinaldi, driving an hour to hit with Venus or Serena for two to three hours, then driving back an hour to my club to give a lesson or to possibly hit with George Bezecny for a couple of hours. By the end of the day, I was ready for bed. I was only able to do this because all that hitting had me in the best shape of my life. If I had been in that kind of shape in college or thereafter, I probably would have had a much more successful tennis-playing career and stayed injury free.

Venus was slow recovering from balls hit out wide to her backhand, and Richard was concerned that she was developing a bad habit of just running back to the middle of the court from that wide position. So, for about two weeks, all we did was footwork drills off both sides of the court. Venus recovered better from her forehand side because she hit mostly from an open stance. The idea was to have her hit more backhands from an open stance in order to give her the same quick recovery she was getting from the open stance forehand. Richard was a stickler about this and any time he looked over and saw Venus crossover instead of push and step, he would stop play and make her do the footwork he wanted for about ten minutes. Some days this could almost bring Venus to tears and one day it did. I had arrived at the practice court a little late one Wednesday, and as we began our warm-up, I could tell that Venus was upset about something. Richard had had her doing the footwork drill before I arrived, and from the amount of perspiration on her shirt, it looked as if she had been at it for quite a while. I called her to the net and asked if everything was all right.

"Do you want to talk about it?" I asked.

"No. I don't know," she answered. "I'll be right back." Then she ran off the court and back into the house. Richard and Serena came out about ten minutes later.

"Dave will you hit with Serena today?" Richard asked.

"Sure. Is Venus ok?" He called me over, out of earshot of Serena.

"Venus is going with her mother for one of those checkups. You know," he said.

"Oh sure."

I had never thought about it before, but Venus and Serena were growing up and becoming young ladies. I was not just dealing with strokes and strategies anymore. Now, emotions came into play at every practice. From then on, I had to watch what I said or how I said it, as one wrong word could turn a dream practice into a nightmare. 'Chalk it up to part of the program when your coaching girls' I thought, as I began to hit with Serena.

I threw away the tournament schedule Richard had told Venus to give me a few months back. Venus had not played any of the ones on my sheet and now Wimbledon was out for this year. We did however, practice on the grass courts for the week of Wimbledon, just like we had the previous year. Venus's grass game was looking like she had grown up in England. She did not fall down once the whole week and her serve was very effective, now that she had added power to her first serve. She was still reluctant to come to the net and Richard was on her case about that.

"How will you ever get to phase two if you do not practice coming in girl? I'll give you a quarter every time you come to the net," he said one day. Well, that was all Venus needed to hear. She and Serena were already learning the art of making money. What a couple of entrepreneurs they were. For example, Serena would specifically bring my favorite flavor of Gatorade to practice and then charge me ten cents per cup to have a drink. And the size of the cups; they were about as big as thimbles. Then, on top of that, I think she was watering down the Gatorade, although she would never admit to it. So Venus seized the opportunity Richard laid in front of her and came to the net on everything. She would serve and volley, chip and charge, attack short balls and even make suicide runs from behind the baseline just to get to the net. When practice was over, she had earned $43.50. Not a bad hourly wage, but it would not be long before an hour's work would earn her hundreds of thousands of dollars. We ended our week on the grass courts with a left-handed battle and a set where we both played in our socks. If you have never played on grass you must experience it and then, if you can, take your shoes off and walk around on the lawn. There is a quiet calmness that just rushes through you and if you close your eyes you will swear you are at Center Court, Wimbledon. Oh the grass!

Up until August of '96, Venus, Serena, and Kathy Rinaldi were just names on the tour. Now they were stars, highlighted in a newsletter I put out every month. Ever since the Tennis Week issue, all my clients wanted to know what the latest news was about the pro players I was coaching. The younger ones wanted to know about Venus and Serena and the older players all knew who Kathy was and some even had a poster of her from when they were junior players. I came up with a one page monthly newsletter called, 'The R.T.T. News Report' (Rineberg Tennis Training). I had just gotten my first computer and thought it would be a fun way to become computer literate and keep my clients up to date with the pros I was coaching. I distributed copies to all the players I coached, including Venus and Serena. I thought that they would get a kick out of seeing their names highlighted throughout the newsletter. My August issue pointed out that both Venus and Kathy would be playing at the tournament in Manhattan Beach on August 12th. I gave a copy to Venus and she commented how she would like to watch Kathy play if she had the time. As it turned out, she never got the chance. Venus would be caught up in a first round battle against Ludmila Richterova that would finally end in Venus's favor 7-6(3), 3-6, 6-2. Kathy had a similar fight on her hands against Debbie Graham, but came up on the short side, losing 6-4, 4-6, 6-1. Then, in a simple twist of fate, the two players ran into each other at the tournament site and they talked. Now Venus had a face to go with the name, and because of their connection with me, she also had a friend on the tour, which for a newcomer can be a cold and lonely place. This is especially true if you are carrying the baggage of being 'the next great player' around your neck, as Venus was. She had already experienced some incidents of other players rooting against her and snubbing her in the locker rooms, but it was only because they were jealous of the attention Venus had received. No wonder Venus would keep to herself at tournaments and retreat to a safe place within. Unfortunately, Kathy would not be at all the tournaments to gradually welcome Venus in with the rest of the girls, but it was a start anyway, and Venus would not forget it.

Venus was in the second round and played the number thirteen seed Linda Wild. Beating Wild meant that she would get to play Steffi Graf in the quarterfinals. She was not going to miss out on that opportunity. She came out and blasted her way past Wild, winning in less than an hour 6-1, 6-2. The buzz around the tournament was that Graf had better not take this young girl, Venus, lightly or she would be going home early. Venus could not help but overhear the expectations and came out against Graf a little nervous. After regaining her composure in the fifth game of the first set, Venus gave Graf all she could handle. The current number one was not always in control, and Venus's power had Graf playing defensively a lot of the time. If not for the unforced errors by Venus during the big points at crucial times of the match, it would have been Venus advancing to the semifinals. Instead she picked up a check for $8,245 for her efforts in reaching the quarterfinals.

Venus's next stop on the west coast was the Toshiba Tennis Classic being held at the beautiful La Costa Resort and Spa. She had to play the qualifying and had a good win in the last round over Barbara Rittner, a top fifty player, 7-5, 6-3. The win put her into the main draw against thirty-eighth ranked Katarina Studenikova of Slovakia. After losing the first set, which again showed Venus's immaturity on big points, she breezed through the second set 6-3 and at 5-4 in the third she had a match point. But Venus had not yet learned the importance of capitalizing on the weakness of an opponent or seizing the moment. Studenikova could not have played a more nervous point, but Venus was the one who committed the error on a relatively easy ball. Venus never recovered, and she lost the set and the match 6-4, 3-6, 7-5. Experience was the last piece of the puzzle that Venus needed to learn in order to build a complete game and she could only get that by being in those types of situations time and time again.

When Venus got back home, Richard again felt it necessary to keep her off the court for a few weeks. He did not want to see her burn out and he also wanted to keep Venus hungry to play more. So that meant the U.S. Open trip was off. Or was it? Kathy Rinaldi called me and said she had received a wildcard into the main draw at the U.S. Open and wanted me to go. I quickly booked an airline ticket and immediately began packing, as I would have to leave the next day in order to get to the tournament site a day before the main draw started. Kathy, like most pros, liked to hit at least once or twice on the actual courts of the tournament to get used to the speed and the bounce. Not every hard court surface will play like the one you have been practicing on. In fact, it is safe to say that no two courts of the same surface are created equal.

The next day, I was walking the grounds of Flushing Meadows; my first U.S. Open. I had never been to New York before and I was now at the biggest grand slam tournament in the world as a tour coach. When I picked up my coach's badge, I felt like I should genuflect in appreciation. The tournament official, who handed me my badge, said that due to the new construction, I would find the coaches' locker room at the old complex on the opposite end of the grounds. This was the last year for the old complex, and taking its place was a modern arena so magnificent, that all the past discomforts for the fans and players would soon be forgotten. It was only fitting that I was experiencing this U.S. Open with a veteran, Kathy Rinaldi, who only knew the old complex and had played in the same Louis Armstrong stadium where all my heroes had played. Just like the old stadium, which still has much to offer, this veteran would try once more to give her fans all that she had left for one more run at a U.S. Open title.

I had always said that New York City was no place for a country boy from Kansas, but after one night of walking the streets, staring at all the people, and marveling at all the lights in Times Square, I now say that everyone should experience New York City at least once in their life. I'm still not sure I would want to live there, but visit there — oh yeah!

Coach Dave Rempel met me in New York City on Sunday, and there was a player's party at the All-Star Café in Times Square that night. We attended, expecting to see maybe two or three of the top players and eat some free food. Much to our surprise, every big-name player you can think of was there, and behind the bar, serving everyone their drinks, was Monica Seles. It was all part of a promo-shoot, as her and Andre Agassi were both investors in the All-Star chain of restaurants. I was standing in a line at the bar when the guy in front of me turned and said, "Hey, what can I get for you guys?" It was Goran Ivanisevic.

"Two of those beers I guess," I said.

He hollered at Seles and she came down and handed us a couple of beers served in baseball bat style bottles. This was so cool. Everyone was so nice. Capriati was there, Sabatini, Muster, Stich, Martin, Majoli and Pierce, just to name a few. 'This is going to be a great week,' I thought to myself as we walked back to our hotel later that night.

The week ended short though, as Kathy went down in her first round match against Florencia Labat. She just could not find her groove, and Labat was playing 'no miss' tennis, getting everything back in play and forcing Kathy into errors. Kathy was pretty upset after the match. I could tell she was not happy with her play, that she had so much more to give, but just ran out of time. I think that deep down she knew this would be her last U.S. Open, and for an athlete like Kathy, who had competed at such a high level for so many years, the end can be a very emotional time. The small crowd that had filled the outside court gave her a standing applause as she exited the court. Her emotions took over and tears filled her eyes and ran down her cheeks. There was a lot of love between her and her fans and that is something that is hard to let go of. My eyes swelled as I watched the whole scene unfold. I was glad to have had the chance to work with such a great champion and I could not help but get caught up in the moment. There was something magical about that first U.S. Open; something that would have me going back to New York City every year, perhaps with Venus or Serena, or both.

THE
BIG
YEAR

XIII

I believe that people are put in each other's lives either for a reason or a season. Whether it is to aid or comfort, inspire or teach, guide or follow; whatever the reason, the only thing that matters is to make the time spent together meaningful. People pass through our lives every day, and it is up to each one of us to figure out if those people are in our lives for a reason or just passing through for a short time, a season.

Venus and Serena were sixteen and fifteen in the fall of 1996, and just like every other teenager, they were trying to figure out just who they were. Every day there was some new question or some new trend that they had a comment about. We would get into long discussions, and sometimes arguments, about why we liked or disliked certain things. Music was the number one topic. Venus was into Nirvana one day and then Rancid the next. She was listening to all kinds of music from all generations, a cynosure of music you might say. Serena stuck to the more recent bands like Rancid, Radiohead, Green Day and every other grunge band you could think of. However, according to the Williams girls, music like bubble gum pop, boy bands, and country was un-cool.

One day, during an October rainstorm, we were all stuck out under the court canopy. I had just gotten back from Hobe Sound, where I had spent the morning surfing some great swells brought in by a storm. The girls had been talking about surfing all summer long, and I had encouraged them to give it a try. They had, and they loved it. Venus was a long boarder, much like me, while Serena liked the short boards for more maneuverability. They had just bought new boards and could not wait to show them to me. We ran from the court to the dog kennel, which was now used to house sporting equipment instead of dogs, and the girls pulled two beautiful boards out from one of the rooms. I was so jealous. My board looked like it had been through World War III and they knew I had been looking for a new one. I could tell that they were very proud of their choices and we talked about what the waves might be like tomorrow. Next to the boards, Venus had a couple of guitars and Serena a set of drums. They said they were taking lessons, which was another teenage whim that they were experiencing, however, that brought on the musical question.

"So Dave, what kind of music do you listen to?" Serena asked.

"Well," I hesitated since I had not ever heard them mention any of my favorite artists, "I like Rick Springfield, Cinderella, Aerosmith. That kind of stuff, oh, and John Denver."

Serena busted out into a hysterical laugh that had her rolling around on the wet ground. Venus tried to hold back, but let out a screaming laugh that shook the trees around us.

In between laughs, Venus commented, "A true 80's boy. I think you need to update."

Serena jumped in, "I don't even know any of those bands and I didn't know Gilligan [Bob Denver] was a singer."

"Okay, okay," I said. "This is coach abuse you know!"

Those girls just loved to make fun of me and have a good laugh. More and more, their personalities were coming to the surface. Being under daddy's control, they had only learned what he felt was important in life. It was time for them to find out for themselves what was important to them. I feel that this was one of the reasons I was in their lives, to bring another perspective and opinion to the table from a totally different background, race, and religion than that of their father. I never tried to influence their opinions, but I always spoke with pride and passion about the things I believed to be important. Whether it was a question about drugs, marriage, boys, girls, sports, cars, surfing, or, of course, music, I always answered honestly because that was all I knew. In those last few months of 1996, I felt the girls and I had stepped beyond the coach/player relationship and became something more meaningful to each other. We had all become friends.

Practice matches between Venus and I were just not the same anymore. The fire and desire to win that we had both always had when we played each other was gone. Now it seemed like Venus was content with splitting sets each time we played. It may have been because she was bored with the same old practice scenario that we had done for the last two years. She had been out on tour so much, that the excitement of preparing for a match at the tournament site against real opponents was far more appealing than practicing at the house in the woods against my imitations of the pro players. We needed to change things a bit and Kathy Rinaldi, who had been away at tournaments for the last five weeks since the U.S. Open, was the answer. After a practice session with Kathy, we were discussing some things when I mentioned that Venus was looking for some practice matches. I didn't know if Kathy would want to practice with Venus, but I felt it was worth mentioning. Kathy jumped at the opportunity. She did not have any tournaments coming up in the near future and wanted some competition. Next, I had to clear it with Richard. I asked him if it would be okay to set up some practice matches between Venus and Kathy and he agreed that it would be good for Venus. So I set it all up, and on the following Wednesday, the former child prodigy Kathy Rinaldi was to play the new, up and coming, Venus Williams in a practice match. I thought Kathy might give Venus some grief if she could play her consistent backcourt game and isolate Venus's forehand.

Kathy had never been out to the house in the woods before, so I met her and she followed me out to the Williams house. After a twenty-minute drive west of Palm Beach and a few dirt roads through the trees we were at the Williams home. When I got out of my car, I looked at Kathy in her car and she was laughing heartily.

"What's so funny?" I asked.

"There is no way you drive out here every day," she said. "I mean, I thought you were playing some sort of trick on me once we got to that last dirt road that was all washed out!"

"Nope this is the compound. See, Venus and Serena are already out there." I pointed across the field to the courts. We walked out to the courts. Venus and Serena immediately stopped hitting and came over. I introduced Kathy to Serena, who had not met her yet. The girls all took it from there and started talking like old friends who had not seen each other in a while. Venus asked Kathy about her last four tournaments and Kathy in turn asked Venus about her schedule for next year. After about fifteen minutes, I had to interject.

"Hey, are we going to play today?" I said jokingly.

Serena said she had homework to do so she could only practice for an hour. We went over to the clay courts while Venus and Kathy stayed to play on the newly resurfaced green and red hard court that had a six foot tall white lettered 'Williams' printed across the wind screens. After an hour's worth of hitting, Serena went to solve some Geometry problems that had been giving her fits, and I took a courtside seat to watch Venus and Kathy play. There were some great rallies, and it was interesting to watch the two styles of play, that were separated by generations, clash.

The powerful open-stanced ground strokes, big serves, and swinging volleys of Venus were being neutralized by Kathy's controlled counter-punching strokes. In the end the power won out though and both players were exhausted from the battle. Richard came out and joined me courtside with his video camera and recorded the last two games of the practice. As the girls exited the court and said their goodbyes, Richard walked over and offered his videotape and advice to Kathy, but she politely declined. It had been a good practice, and as Kathy and I walked across the open field towards our cars, she expressed an interest in doing more practices with the girls. In the following months, I tried to set up additional practices sessions, but after a few rain-outs and some schedule changes, 1996 was over.

I believe Kathy was just passing through Venus's life for a season, and that she had come to give Venus a look at how the game was once played and a new respect for those who had played the game before her. Venus said that she admired Kathy's determination and work ethic, which she had displayed throughout their practice match, and even commented on how she needed more of those qualities. It was apparent that Kathy had gained Venus' respect, and that is not always an easy thing to obtain from the younger generation, but at this time Venus was more open to outside influences.

XIV

1997 was to be a coming together year for Venus and a coming out year for Serena. I had thought 1996 could have been much better if the year would have been planned. There was no rhyme or reason to the tournaments Richard allowed Venus to play. While she was skipping all around, gaining a few ranking points, Martina Hingis was playing a full schedule and moving up the rankings fast.

As a tour player, life revolves around the four major tournaments: The Australian Open in January, The French Open in May,

Wimbledon in June/July, and the U.S. Open in August/September. Connecting those four majors are smaller tournaments that players use for training and as stepping-stones to higher rankings. A good plan, set up early in the year, can help a player progress towards their ultimate goals. As players improve, they will perform at higher levels and move closer towards their goals. They often find that the difference between succeeding and failing lies within the preparation of their plan.

My father, who had been a star athlete at St. Louis University and a coach himself thereafter, always taught me that 'preparation is the key to success', and that a person is responsible for his own actions. I tried to pass that coaching advice on to my players, having them take responsibility for their games by writing out a plan to put themselves on the hook. A written plan is as good as a business contract. It reminds the player, each and every day, of everything they have to do in order to fulfill their part. It is important to remember to be realistic when you set goals within your plan though. If a player is ranked one hundred in the world, they should not aspire to be number one in the world and win three out of four majors within one year. That is being unrealistic. In order to set realistic goals, a player must have an intimate knowledge of themselves that they can only get from experience and hard work.

If Venus had said at the beginning of the year that she was going to get to the finals of a major tournament, then most everyone would have said that that was unrealistic, because she had not yet played in any major, nor had she been in a tournament final. She needed more experience. By playing smaller tournaments throughout the year, she might then learn what it would take to win a major. If she on the other hand, had said that she wanted to move up at least one hundred spots in the rankings, then I think we all would have agreed that that was realistic.

Richard agreed with me about setting goals and said that Venus had already told him that she wanted to be in the top thirty by the end of the year, but he disagreed with me on planning out her schedule to peak for the majors, and said that Venus was still only going to play a minimum number of tournaments. As far as the majors went, it would depend on her homework and her grades. I am sure that Richard had a plan of his own, he just was not sharing it with me or anyone else.

Venus's serve was stronger than ever when the Indian Wells tournament rolled around in early march. This would be her first tournament of the year and my expectations were high. In practices she had started to place her powerful first serve, which was now occasionally reaching the 110mph mark. She was ranked 211th on the computer and had to get a wildcard to play the qualifier in order to get into the main draw. She won both of her qualifying matches and then two main draw matches. This set up a match against ninth-ranked Iva Majoli of Croatia. Venus had yet to beat a top ten opponent and Majoli was seeded fifth. Venus came out swinging all or nothing on every shot. She took the first set 7-5, but then dropped the second set 3-6. It would have to be decided with a third set and Venus's history against top-ranked players in third sets was very shaky. She played the third set with no fear and her serve really came through for her. After some of her typical unforced errors on big points, she found herself with a match point against her on her serve at 4-5. She did what she knew best, which was to go for broke. She served a 109 mph ace, erasing the match point and then evening out the set at 5-5. Majoli self destructed after that, serving up a double fault at 0-40, giving Venus the chance to serve out the match, which she did on her third match point. Venus was so happy she jumped up and down at the net, waiting to shake Majoli's hand. As she jumped, a row of the beads she wore in her hair broke loose and scattered across the court to be swept up as souvenirs for some of the ball kids.

In the post match interview, Venus said that she had played nowhere near her ability. "I wasn't attacking the short balls. The high balls, I wasn't taking those out of the air. And on the return of serves, I wasn't attacking those. It was nothing near what I can do and I know that if I can go out there and just go for broke, you guys will see a real match."

Venus's confidence was back, and she did a bit of self-promoting to the press, which some of the players did not like, but she would have to do more than talk against her next opponent, Lindsay Davenport, if she expected to stay in the tournament.

Serena had also made the trip to Indian Wells and this time not as a spectator. She and Venus were playing together in their first WTA doubles event. Entered as a wildcard team, they upset the eighth- seeded team of Conchita Martinez and Patricia Tarabini in the first round, then in the second round they came back from a set down to defeat Asa Carlsson and Anne-Gaelle Sidot. That put them in the quarterfinals against Lindsay Davenport and Natalia Zvereva. Serena was playing great in her first event. The irony was, that neither she nor Venus had a clue about playing doubles, they were both just out there, swinging away and chasing down every ball like a couple of singles players. But they were overpowering their opponents and out-hustling them and their athleticism had some of the other girls intimidated. I have always believed that Venus and Serena could have chosen any sport and been successful. They were just too athletic not to do well.

Back in the singles event, Venus gave Davenport all she could handle for three sets. Davenport had everything to lose, and after blowing two match points in the second set, her attitude became negative and her strokes tentative. Venus took full advantage, winning the second set and jumping to a 4-2 third set lead. Venus showed her inexperience though, and made some unforced errors on the big points. When Davenport had her out of position, Venus would go for a winner instead of keeping the ball in play. Her serve reached a career high of 113mph, but it failed her toward the end of the set. In addition, Davenport started hitting deeper and took control of the match, winning the third set in a tiebreaker. It was a disappointment for Venus and it carried over into her doubles match with Serena, which they lost to Davenport and her partner as well. In the post match interview, one question really summed up Venus's approach to her game at the time.

Q: "You started serve and volleying in the second set. How come you abandoned that when it worked for those couple of points?"

Venus: "Because I didn't want to do that anymore."

When the girls got back home, we had a few days of practice before Venus would be playing in the Lipton championships. The Lipton was held in Key Biscayne, Florida, just an hour and a half drive from the house in the woods. Serena was the one who was excited to practice upon returning. She had had a positive first time experience on the tour and could not wait to get out there fulltime. She had some definite things she wanted to work on. Her serve needed more power, her return game needed to be more aggressive, and her down-the-line shots needed more pace. She had all this written down and showed it to me before practice. It was a good plan, but there was one element missing, namely self-discipline.

Venus could not stop talking about how she had let Davenport push her around, especially towards the end of the match. She felt she should have won and so did I. My suggestion to her was that she needed to work on situations and closing out sets.

"We need to play sets starting at 5-4, your serve, and play games with you up 40-30. Learning to play smart in those types of situations will make you a stronger player mentally. But you will have to discipline yourself to play the right shots during those times and out-work your opponent to achieve success."

The girls' lack of self-discipline had an effect on their games. Until now, they had been coasting on natural talent with minimal effort. I had never seen either of the girls push themselves further than they believed they could go. Venus's losses had all been to those players who had a great deal of self-discipline and showed it in their games. Sure, most of those players were the veterans and top ranked players, who had learned through experience what self-discipline was, and Venus just did not have that experience to draw from, but the sooner she learned, the quicker she would start winning those tough matches. I believed self-discipline to be a key factor in Venus or Serena becoming the best players in the world. There have not been many number one players, on either the men or women's tour, who got there without disciplining something in their game or life. I think even outside the world of sports, success is achieved most often through discipline. At this time, Serena was much less disciplined than Venus. One day, Serena was eating some fast food right before practice and Venus got on her case about her poor eating habits. I agreed with Venus and together we lectured Serena about taking responsibility for her actions.

Serena asked me what I thought self-discipline was, and I could not wait to answer.

I said, "self-discipline is saying to yourself that you will not just expect the least from yourself anymore, that you will strive to get the best and only the best from yourself in whatever you do."

Serena nodded in agreement.

XV

The Lipton Championship was one of the tournaments that had always been on my travel list. Because it was basically a local tournament for both Venus and I, it was very easy to arrange practices and match warm-ups. I knew my way around, because I had been attending the tournament since 1989. The tournament had a beautiful stadium and because it was both a men and women's event, it carried the same vibe as a grand slam tournament. In fact, many people, including the players, referred to it as the fifth major.

Venus's previous results at Indian Wells had some of the critics changing their views of her chances at the Lipton. She was becoming a player that could get hot and wreck a draw. *Seeds beware with Williams in the draw* read a local headline on the tournament. Her first round match was on the stadium court and it drew an almost capacity crowd. Venus began in Florida right where she had left off in California, attacking and swinging big off both sides. The match was 7:30pm prime time, and it was a cool breezy evening as could be expected in South Florida in March. Serena and I both had sweat suit jackets on as we took our seats in the players box. Richard had brought his video camera and planned to film the match. Venus looked up to the box a few times during the warm-up. She seemed a little nervous and was flying balls beyond the baseline already. She was playing number 526 Ginger Helgeson Nielsen. She played an up and down match that had as much excitement in the stands as it did on the court.

During one point, a lady in the crowd screamed so loud that it caught everyone's attention. The players stopped. Then more people screamed, and a whole section on the west side stood up and started jumping all about. Apparently, a rat had appeared from out of one of the flower planters and it was scurrying about the stands. The match had completely stopped, and the players went to their chairs, as the stadium staff had to chase down and finally box the rat. Venus had won the first set convincingly 6-1, but dropped the second, during the rat ordeal, 4-6. Once the excitement died down, she regrouped and won the third set and the match 6-1, 4-6, 6-3. The press conference questions afterwards concerned everything from the match, the rat, her homework and even a question about her mystery coach.

Q: "How did you feel about the rat?"

Venus: "The rat? That was very odd. I really didn't know what was going on. Actually, I thought it was some type of creature. I guess I figured it was a rat. I thought it was some type of mouse, not a rat."

Q: "What are your favorite subjects in school?"

Venus: "My favorite is psychology, maybe. What else do I like?

French. I'm not the best French speaker, mostly mute. I can say hello and goodbye. I can't hold a conversation after two minutes."

Pretty basic questions up until this point. It was my first press conference with Venus, and I was about to leave because it was so boring, when a question that caught my attention came.

Q: "Do you have one or two coaches right now that you are working with?"

Venus: "Just one, yeah. Usually I don't get too much coaching anymore. Well, sometimes I do, sometimes I don't. It depends.

Q: "Whom do you work with now?"

Venus: "I work with my father, and I work with Dave Rineberg, see him."

She pointed across the room at me. I was shocked. This was the first time Venus had given credit to anyone besides her father. A couple of members of the media grabbed me after Venus had left and asked me some basic questions about my background and how long I had been with the Williams'. It was all pretty exciting. Her mentioning me at all, showed me how close we had become. The roller coaster ride had just made an upward turn and was starting to climb again.

Next up for Venus was a player who was no newcomer to the tour, Jennifer Capriati. Capriati was still in a comeback mode from her burnout departure from the game back in 1993. Since her return, her results were very mixed and she had not yet won a tournament. In spite of this, all the players still considered her one of the best ball strikers on tour, and if she could get her mental game back, she would once again be a threat at any tournament. Capriati looked nervous, but so did Venus, and together they had a terrible warm-up. Neither player could hit two balls in a row. Venus took a 5-1 lead in the first set, which looked a lot like the warm-up — sloppy. Instead of closing out the set, Venus let Capriati back in, and the set went to a tiebreaker. Both players gave up early mini-breaks and then Venus hit a couple of winners and took the tiebreaker 7-5. However, a pattern was starting to develop in Venus's matches. She would win the first set, only to lose focus and give up the second set, and then have to battle for her life in the third set. Capriati won the second set, however this time, Venus played a good third set and Capriati helped her win by double faulting some games away. The win put Venus into the next round and up against another child prodigy, the up and coming, number one player Martina Hingis.

The game plan against Hingis was to attack her weak serve and try to come to the net more. Richard was very blunt with Venus right before the match. He wanted her at the net whenever possible and inside the baseline on every ground stroke. Hingis won the coin toss and elected to serve. Venus broke her right away and then held serve. Hingis served again and Venus broke again. She was up 3-0 and in cruise control. Venus was sticking to her game plan. She was attacking Hingis's 75 mph serves and overpowering the five foot six inch Swiss with deep penetrating strokes from inside the baseline. The red, white, and blue beads in her hair were clacking with each shot, and she let out a grunt on every ball impact, which made it seem like she was hitting even harder. Venus was into it and then a couple of forehands flew long. Then a backhand went into the bottom of the net. On the next shot, Venus stumbled, but recovered to hit a winner. Then she cracked a serve at 106 mph to win her serve, and after that she stepped even farther inside the baseline to return Hingis's serve. Hingis kept her poise though, and once she gauged Venus's pace, she began changing the rhythm and displaying an arsenal of finesse shots that threw Venus's timing off. Venus lost the first set 6-4 and then lost the second set in eighteen minutes, 6-2. Hingis's counterpunching had Venus searching for plan B. The problem was that there was no plan B, and her power game (plan A) had self destructed or been immobilized.

In the press conference, Venus was in no mood to talk. Her answers were quick and sometimes rude. Hingis on the other hand opened her press conference by flicking one of Venus's beads into the crowd of reporters saying, "A nice present for you." A rivalry was born. But when asked if Hingis was her rival now, Venus dismissed it and said, "Serena and I will be the ones fighting to be the best players in the world." Richard then cut the questioning short, saying it was late and Venus had to study. We all hustled out to the player transportation area to get our cars. The Lipton had a valet service for the players, and while we waited, some reporters trying to get a few extra quotes caught up with Richard.

The next morning I would read that Richard had told them that he was glad Venus lost, and that he was in no rush for Venus to succeed, as long as she was happy. Serena was the one Richard claimed every girl had better watch out for, not Venus. The article went on to quote Richard, "Serena will be better than Venus. She's more aggressive. She has a better all-around game." After reading that article, two things occurred to me. One was that Venus was not happy and two, the hype was starting to build again. This time it would be for Serena.

XVI

My second death threat came a few days after the tournament. My first had been a phone call to my home one night back in 1995. I remember I was sitting on my apartment floor, stretching out after a long day's workout. The phone rang and I answered it. The man on the other end said, "You think you're good enough to be hitting with Venus Williams? I think you better just walk away before you get seriously hurt or worse." I felt fear race through my body, and my jaw must have locked up because I did not say anything. I just hung up the phone. The next day, I had gone to the police and talked to an officer about the incident. I asked him what I should do and whether I should involve my family and friends. He suggested that we wait and see if this was an isolated incident, but that if it happened again, we would then follow procedures. He also said not to worry my family and friends about it unless the man had targeted them as well. It was better to have less people involved at this point. So, I did not tell my friends, I did not tell my family, I did not tell anyone. Being an introvert, I just kept the worry, stress, and strain all to myself. I remember that during that time, I was looking for a new community to move into. I picked the one farthest away, hoping to put some distance between this psychopath and me.

The second threat was different in that it was directed at me, but also involved Venus. The voice on the phone said, "I don't like you hitting with that n...!. Stop or someone might die." The person hung up. The threat came on my cell phone, which led me to believe that whoever it was did not have my new home phone number. The next morning, I told Richard about the phone call. He just seemed to shrug it off as nothing and said that this sort of thing had happened to him and Venus and Serena numerous times. That was one reason for his move out to the house in the woods and for his keeping practices closed to outsiders. I also talked with a friend of mine, a police officer whom I played basketball with once a week. He said he would be happy to bodyguard for Venus and me at any of the local events. I told him that we had bodyguards at the Lipton, and that Venus would be in Europe next. "Nothing in the states till August." He suggested that I arranged for protection at all the events.

Was this how it was going to be? Had Venus reached such superstar status that bodyguards would be needed everywhere she went? I was hoping that this was just an act of some bigoted person, venting his bias and not a real threat. It angered me more than anything that people in this day and age could still be so hateful. It definitely was not going to make me quit working with Venus. In fact, it just made my commitment even stronger. A third threat was still to come.

All of this must have started Richard thinking, because at our first practice back at the house he called me off the court. "Dave, I know I am not paying you near what you are worth. Here's two hundred for the tournament and I'll have Venus write you a bonus check for ten thousand at the end of the month," he said. Then he pulled a couple of Venus's checks out of his golf cart to show me. They were large checks from Reebok for several hundred thousand dollars. He said they were just royalty checks and that there were more on top of that. Why was he showing me these checks? He said Venus had too much money already and that he was thinking of having her retire in eighteen months. This was the first time I heard the early retirement routine, but it would not be the last. Just another one of Richard's 'tall tales', as I liked to call them. The two hundred dollars he gave me did not excite me. Two months before, he had said that he would pay me a thousand dollars per tournament week. However, the bonus check of ten thousand dollars sounded much better.

Venus played the Amelia Island tournament the next week and had another good win, beating top ranked player Chandra Rubin. Reebok was getting excited about Venus's results, and upon her return, a commercial shoot was set up at a local tennis facility in Delray Beach. Richard told me to wear my newest Reebok gear because I was going to be in the commercial. Okay, so I had still not received my bonus check or been fully paid for the tournament. Did I really believe I was going to be in a commercial that would be shown all across the nation? Of course I did. Remember, I was just a naive Kansas boy.

I showed up at the site and the crew immediately gave me a new shirt. A make-up artist blotched my face a few times and another guy walked to one side of the court and told me I would be hitting balls to Venus's backhand side. 'This is really going to happen,' I thought. I began to get very nervous. The first couple of balls Venus hit to me I shanked into the stadium seats. When the rigor mortis left my arm, we got some rallies going, and then the extra lighting came on, making it feel as if I was under a heat lamp. Sweat began poring down my face and my navy shirt became soaked. The shoot stopped so Venus could get a drink. Someone came over to me and gave me a new shirt and a bottle of water. "Am I going to be in this thing?" I asked, but before I got an answer, the shoot started again. I glanced over to the cameras and noticed that they were not turning my way at all. In fact, the furthest they turned was to the net and then back to Venus. Okay, so I was not going to make it into the commercial, but the whole Hollywood scene sure gave me a charge.

The next day, Reebok was at the house in the woods for another picture shoot. Serena and I hit, while Venus spent two hours under the lights again. This was the glamorous side of athletics. The commercials, picture shoots, autograph sessions, all the things that come with fame and right now Venus was famous. When I was younger, I wanted to be a rock star, but after those two days I said the heck with that. Besides, rock stars have to wear black all the time, don't they?

Venus would be leaving for Europe in May and we had to get her hitting more consistent if she was going to get any good results on the slow, red clay. Right now, Venus was a three-ball hitter before she would go for a winner or make an error. She needed to be a ten-ball hitter. In order to do that, she was going to have to become more patient, and drills were my answer to that problem. I sat in one corner of the court and hit heavy topspin and after Venus hit ten to that corner I would switch sides. We did this for about an hour each day. She was about a six-ball hitter by the time she left for France, but was still very impatient in constructing points. Her serve was still inconsistent because of her grip, but her power had increased. She could now hit a serve as fast as a Ferrari. Venus had a way of gauging her serve speeds by comparing

Serena, myself and Venus looking strong and happy

Venus proudly showing how she has outgrown me

Serena and I on the practice court at the 1998 U.S. Open

The Williams girls enjoying a
moment at the 1998 U.S. Open

Pat Egan and I enjoying a sunny day
out at Flushing Meadows

Night match at the U.S. Open...
Venus' favorite

One of my rare autographs, being
given at the U.S. Open...

Venus and Oracene after a night practice at
the Lipton — The court attendant has me
searching my bag for a souvenir practice ball

'Bigger than life'— Reebok ad
featuring Venus during the U.S. Open

Venus at the Reebok clinic on the streets of
New York City

Venus holding the champion's trophy in front of
a sellout crowd at the Lipton Championship

Venus and myself exiting the practice court at the
Lipton — Richard taking a smoke break behind us

George Bezecny, myself and Dave Rempel training in Florida

Working on Venus' serve on practice court 2 of
the U.S. Open (next to Arthur Ashe Stadium)

Hitting with Serena on practice court 1 at the U.S.
Open — by her early racquet preparation you can
tell she already knows where the ball is going

Venus, myself and Serena enjoying a
laugh — at my expense, I'm sure!

Venus, my sister Charlotte, my mom Barbara,
and Serena at the Williams house in the woods

Dave Rempel and I practicing in our
favorite bands' T-shirts

Coach Dave Rempel taking a break at the
house in the woods — notice the cars
abandoned in the field

A 1999 pre-Australian Open practice
on the hard courts

Kathy and I preparing for
the French Open in 1996

Tammy Whittington and I working out at
the Deerfield Beach Tennis Center, 1993

Me with two Venus fans —
my nephew Daniel and niece Audrey

11 year old Serena and 12 year old
Venus with Jim Tierney at the
Deerfield Beach Tennis Center

George Bezecny and I displaying our 2000 State
Doubles and National 35 Claycourt doubles titles

them to certain cars or trucks. I laughed the first time she aced me and said, "That wasn't even a Ferrari, that was just a semi-truck."

"What are you talking about girl?"

"My serving speed order goes: Jeep, pick-up truck, SUV, semi-truck, Porsche, Lamborghini, and Ferrari."

This just goes to show you what was on this sixteen year old's mind. She would have her drivers permit soon and deciding what kind of car to get was a very big deal.

She left for France on May 21st. This was her first trip across the ocean and she would be gone until after Wimbledon, a little more than a month. Venus's European vacation was all about gaining experience. Her mother, Oracene, and Serena went along for the same reason. Getting used to the time change, booking hotels, getting around cities, and oh yeah, playing matches on the red clay were all new things to be experienced. What a great age to be traveling to Europe. Open minded and feeling freedom that you may never have again in your life. Boy, was I jealous.

The French open would be Venus's first major tournament. Because of her good results so far in 1997, she would not have to qualify. She won her first round in typical form, cruising in the first set 6-2, losing the second set in a tiebreaker, but then pulling out a close fought third set 7-5. The win moved her into the second round of a major, and at this point, that was huge for her. In the second round, Venus was up against the veteran French player Natalie Tauziat. Tauziat was not as gifted physically as Venus, but she was one of the smartest competitors on tour. She could mix up her game to fit any situation and loved to come to the net at every opportunity. Venus had her chances, but the veteran was too crafty and Venus fell 5-7, 6-3, 7-5. Not bad for her first time on the slow red clay. I always figured this would be Venus's toughest surface because of the patience and discipline needed to win a point.

The next stop on tour was Eastbourne and the next surface was grass. On grass, patience is not as important, because any shot hit powerful enough will skip or slide and become virtually un-hittable for an opponent. Venus definitely had the power, and if she could master the footwork needed, anything could happen. To help her get some experience on the grass, Venus did not accept a wildcard that was offered into the main draw. Instead, she played the qualifier, hoping to tune her grass court play before the tournament's main draw. Her first grass match ever was against Wiltrud Probst from Germany. It was the first round of qualifying, and Venus won it easily 6-0, 6-0. She won her next two qualifying matches with a walkover in the second round against Barabanschikova and then in straight sets 6-3, 6-4 in the final round against Saeki. Venus was overpowering on both her serves and her ground strokes. She did slip a few times, which was all part of mastering the footwork, but it did not deter her from occasionally coming into the net or from chasing after every ball.

In the main draw at Eastbourne, Venus drew Chandra Rubin in the first round. She had lost to Rubin two months earlier at Amelia Island in straight sets, which included getting bageled in the second set. But that was on clay and Venus would prove that power was queen on the grass by avenging her loss at Amelia Island with a straight set win of 6-4, 6-4. That was four consecutive wins, and if not for three being qualifying matches, Venus would have been more than halfway through the tournament. She was into the second round though, and now had a chance to avenge a loss against Natalie Tauziat that she had suffered just two weeks earlier at the French Open. Tauziat again showed Venus that her experience was far superior to Venus's power game. Venus pushed her to three sets, but just could not seem to find her big serve to help her hold in the third set. Tauziat got the break and won the match 6-3, 5-7. 6-4.

I opened the paper each morning as part of my routine to get the updates on Venus's pre-Wimbledon tournament results. Everyone was asking me what I thought Venus's chances were at Wimbledon. I had a standard answer that I used, which went back to a practice Venus and I had had on a grass court about a year earlier. After hitting all day on the perfectly manicured grass courts of a Palm Beach country club, Venus and I were sitting on a bench talking and I asked her,

"So, which major do you want to win the most?"

"Wimbledon? Yeah, definitely Wimbledon the most," she answered. "I just love running around on a grass court. It's fun. I feel like I could run all day."

That was enough for me. Anytime a player enjoys a tournament so much that it becomes fun, they become a threat. So, when people asked me how I thought Venus would do at Wimbledon, I always said, "She's got a great chance of winning. She loves the grass."

Expectations were high for Venus's first Wimbledon. Everyone at the Deerfield Tennis Center crowded around a nineteen inch TV to watch her first round, which had her up against Magdalena Grzybowska from Poland. A great draw, as Grzybowska was not a veteran to the tour and had about as much experience on grass as Venus. A quick win might get Venus through the nerves of her first Wimbledon, and the grass court success she was having might steam roll into something bigger, like a championship. Venus had big plans for her first Wimbledon experience and before she left, she had said that there would be a surprise and that I should watch for it. As soon as she walked out on court, I noticed her big surprise. She had replaced the red, white, and blue beads in her hair with green and purple ones, which are the Wimbledon colors. It may sound trivial to some people, but to replace those beads is a big deal. It takes around three hours to get them all in and positioned correctly. Venus was becoming very meticulous about fashion, and I am sure she spent even longer than that getting those beads just right. I just hoped she would be as meticulous about her game.

Both players looked nervous in the first set and it really came down to who was not going to make the error, as opposed to who was going to hit the winner. Venus held out and took the first set 6-4. However, she never really looked comfortable and her serve was giving her fits again. Then, for some reason, she started isolating Grzybowska's backhand side when the scouting report was clear that the forehand side was the weaker of the two. Grzybowska took full advantage of the situation, hitting winners and angles that made Venus look slow and out of position. Venus should have made adjustments and gone to plan B, but there was still no plan B, and she continued to hit to Grzybowska's backhand side until the match was over.

The headlines the next day read, *Venus out of orbit.*

XVII

I called Richard, who had stayed at home, to see if he wanted to discuss the match or put together a game plan for Venus and Serena's practices when they returned in a few days. As usual, he was unreachable and would not return any of the phone messages I left on his answering machine. He had a new voice message at this time, which greeted me with the shocking words: "Any black man who marries a white woman should be hung at sundown. Richard Williams." At first, I did not know if I should leave a message. What was he insinuating here? Was he against mixed marriages or was it the white woman that had him upset? I was white, so was he mad at me? I hung up. By the fourth time I called, I just figured it to be another 'Richardism', which is what I called any quote or phrase Richard used that no one else understood, and left my message.

Richard did not always travel to Venus's tournaments back then. He was very animated in stating that Venus had to learn on her own without him always being around. He was not going to sit in the stands and turn his head from side to side. He had more important things to do, he would say. The press hounded him and Venus both about why he was not around, but Venus always dodged the question and Richard was becoming more and more unavailable for comment. Venus and Serena were not on their own anyway. In fact, they were in the best care possible since their mother was acting coach at all the tournaments. If Richard was the head coach and I was the hitting coach, then their mother, acted as their psychological, mental toughness, and morality coach.

I had not seen much of their mother up until this point, but as Richard's business affairs took him away from practice sessions, Oracene started sitting in. She was always telling the girls to be strong and not to get down on themselves. If Venus was hanging back at the baseline too much, Oracene would yell at her to get to the net. If Serena tossed a racquet in frustration, Oracene would reprimand her immediately, telling her, "Champions don't do things like that." She was teaching her two daughters how to be strong, proud women. I think she was afraid for them, that if they were not strong enough mentally, the life of a tennis pro would get the best of them. The girls may have gotten their athletic talent from their father, but they got their inner strength from their mother. Practices might now include Richard or Oracene or both, myself, Gerard or Dave Rempel, an accountant, a lawyer and maybe another sister or two. The support group was stronger than ever.

Oracene had the toughest job of anyone. Being a religious woman, she feared that her daughters' humility would be stolen away by the thieves of adoration. She not only had to raise two girls into womanhood, but also two clean minds into a not so clean world. She was tough on the girls and when they did not walk proud she told them, when they did not say thank you she scolded them, and when they showed signs of not believing in themselves she corrected them, telling them they could do it. In an interview in 1997 about Venus, Oracene said, "Venus matured a lot in the last six months, but I do not think she is mature enough. This is scary to me, the fast life, the craziness. There is a risk that Venus will idolize herself and not become aware of who she is and who she is not." Just as Richard was not going to let the nay-sayers of tennis disrupt his grand plan for the girls, Oracene was not going to let the world take advantage of her girls nor take away their belief in God and themselves that she had taken pains to instill in them. So far so good!

Venus and Serena returned to the States and took a couple of weeks off to have some fun. We were back to practice on July 14th. Venus hit great her first day back and in between her stories of Wimbledon and The French Open, she was giving me all I could handle. She still had the purple and green beads she had worn at Wimbledon in her hair, and they clacked away with every hit. During practice, one of the rubber bands, which held her beads back off her face, broke and she went inside to try and find another one. After ten minutes of searching, she came out and said she would have to stop because she could not hit with the beads smacking her in the face all the time. I searched through my tennis bag and came up with an industrial strength rubber band that had come wrapped around my string packages. Serena, peeking over from the other court, saw it and said she wanted one like that too. I dug up another one and the girls raved. "Alright Dave, You're the man!" I had been afraid of losing my cool status, but apparently not. After that, I made sure that I always carried extra rubber bands in my tennis bag.

Venus and I had two weeks to workout before she would be leaving for California to play tournaments in San Diego and Manhattan Beach. She needed to work on consistency, big point play, and serves. Every day, Richard had Venus throwing racquets out in the field next to the courts. He was trying to get her used to more of a backhand grip on her serve. I worked on Venus's point play when we played sets. I pointed out each time there was a big point, reminding her to not be hasty in her approach to the situation. Venus worked on the consistency of her ground strokes and was trying to come to the net more. She definitely was maturing and had a much better sense of when to and when not to go for it.

In that first week, she worked harder than I had seen her work in the last two months. She was chasing down everything, moving her feet on every shot and jumping all over any short ball I gave her. She was feeling pretty confident by the end of that week, and that was when she made the big statement to her mother. Oracene was sitting under the court canopy next to our court and had just encouraged Venus to retrieve one of my better drop shots.

"You know there's not a single drop shot that I can't get," Venus said with typical teenage cockiness.

"If you think you can get to any drop shot," her mother responded, "how come you can't get to any ball?"

"Alright Oracene!" I said. Once again she was working on Venus's attitude. Venus had no retort.

We continued our practice match and at every opportunity I hit a drop shot. Sure enough, there was Venus chasing it down. That scenario continued until dinnertime. The following week, practices were much lighter. Richard had already left for California and whenever he was not around, the girls liked to dog it a bit. But that was okay, because Venus had another stretch of tournament travel ahead of her. To help keep it light, I brought my mom and sister, who were visiting from Kansas, out to watch practice on the last day before Venus left. The girls were great to both my mom and sis, showing them around and offering them refreshments. They even brought over chairs for them to sit on while they watched. Oracene came out to the courts for a while and had a conversation with my mom. Later my mom told me that Oracene had said that they were glad to have me working with their girls. I tried to get my sister out on the court since she was a great college player, but she was too shy and did not have anything but sandals to wear. Venus offered her a pair of her tennis shoes, but to no avail. Before they left, the jokester Venus could not help but get one good dig in on me. She asked my mom, "So, is Dave's dog back home named Toto?" My mom laughed, but not as hard as Venus and Serena. "Coach abuse once again!" I cried.

In San Diego, Venus again entered the qualifying tournament in order to get more match play. She cruised through all three rounds, not dropping a set. She faced Florencia Labat in the first round of the main draw. Labat was the steady player who had ruined Rinaldi's final U.S. Open singles bid in 1996. She had no real weapons and Venus beat her easily, 6-3, 6-2, in a little over an hour. This set up another meeting with the current number one, Martina Hingis, whom Venus had played and lost to in March at the Lipton Tennis Tournament.

Hingis was having a great year. She had won the Australian Open, lost in the finals of the French Open, won Wimbledon and had taken over the tour as the number one player. She had such style and grace that it was hard to believe that she was only sixteen years old. Her game was totally opposite Venus's. They were like fire and ice. Hingis was finesse minded and Venus was a baseline basher. Hingis' five foot six inch frame did not look like it could hold out against Venus's six foot one inch athletically sculptured build. But it did, time and time again. When Venus would hit one of her laser-like ground strokes into one of the corners, Hingis was there, waiting with a response that either put Venus in handcuffs or out to position. Hingis won in straight sets and again down played the media hype that Venus was a future threat to her new world reign of the women's tour.

Venus had played five matches in San Diego, adding needed experience to her overall game. Every time she lost, the media was quick to point out her lack of junior tournament play, citing inexperience as the reason for her downfalls. Whether or not that had anything to do with it was a mute point. It would be something she would just have to learn to live with, because it would keep coming up after each loss.

In Manhattan Beach, Venus accepted a wildcard offered to play in the main draw. Her first opponent was a seasoned veteran, Ann Grossman, who had qualified for the main draw by winning two rounds. Venus overpowered Grossman at the start by hitting first serves that averaged 105mph. She blasted ground stroke winners past Grossman like she was standing still. Venus won the first set at love. In the second set it looked as though Venus was going to slip into her usual pattern of winning the first set and then losing the second, when she got down an early break. Nevertheless, this time she regained control of her ground strokes and managed an erratic serve to win the second set and the match, 6-0, 6-3.

Venus's next opponent was a young player from Germany, Anka Huber. Huber was having her best year on tour, and she was another baseline basher, the type of player, who had a big western forehand and a two handed backhand. Venus did not have quite as much of a western forehand, and the scouting report on Huber said that her forehand side would break down under pressure. Huber was a streaky player, which meant that when she was hot she could roll, but if a player hung in there long enough she was prone to making errors. This was similar to the scouting report on Venus's game.

The match played out just as the scouting report read. Huber was hot for a while, then Venus got hot for a while. Huber made a lot of forehand errors and so did Venus. It was almost as if each player was playing a mirror image of herself. In the end, it came down to confidence and Huber had it, winning the first set in a tiebreaker and the second set 6-4. What do you think the media said the next day? Venus lacked tournament experience, of course.

Toronto was the next stop on Venus's 1997 tour and it would be her debut in Canada. She was in the main draw and played a qualifier in the first round. However, the hard courts Venus had been playing on the last three weeks were taking a toll on her growing knees. She went into the match with soreness just below the kneecap. She tried to play through the pain, and in an attempt to reduce the amount of pounding on her knees she tried to end the points quickly by being overly aggressive. This led to very fast sets. She would either hit a quick winner or make an unforced error. Unfortunately, she made more unforced errors and lost the match 6-1, 1-6, 6-1.

XVIII

Venus was back home in Florida the next day. She was taking summer courses and had a lot of homework to catch up on, so we did not practice right away. Richard had not yet said whether he was going to let Venus play the U.S. Open. With her knees bothering her, he was definitely leaning towards not letting her play.

I hit with Serena for most of the week, but by Friday Venus was feeling better and had caught up on all her homework. She was anxious to play sets against me and I think she was hoping to finally win two sets off me, which she had not been able to do up to this point. I had been practicing a lot with George Bezecny while she was away, so my game was solid. I spun the racquet for serve like I always did, asking Venus if she wanted to choose P or D. She had for as long as I had known her always chosen P, so you can imagine my surprise when she said D.

"What did you just say," I said.

"D," she repeated.

"You never in the history of the world have ever chosen D before. What's up?"

"I think it's time I make some changes," she said.

I looked at her through one eye and then out the other. She was smiling. All this time, she had been reluctant to change anything, including her serve grip, her forehand grip, and her patience, just to name a few. She had always resisted change in these areas. Was she now so enlightened that she could see that change was needed in order to be successful? Losing tends to make players search within themselves for an antidote. Venus was tired of experiencing defeat, often snatched from the jaws of victory.

We played one set, and it lasted over an hour. Venus was being patient and consistent. We had some fifteen ball rallies and almost every game went to deuce. We worked on her serve at the end, and even did some footwork drills. With this attitude adjustment, Venus was a new player. I thought she should play the U.S. Open, and I told Richard.

"It's already decided that she will not play. Her knees need a rest. If I change my mind, I'll let you know," he said.

In order to play, I knew Richard had to let the WTA know by Monday. Therefore, I decided to wait until then and just ask Venus if she was going to play. On Monday, Serena came out to practice, but Venus and Richard were nowhere to be found. I asked Serena if Venus was playing the U.S. Open and she said she did not know. That night I tried to call Richard on his cell phone, only to get his latest message asking everyone to please send money to a man in California, who was a crack addict and needed cash. There was just a few days left before the U.S. Open, and when I drove out to the house the next day for practice, but found it deserted. There were no cars in the driveway and all the blinds were shut. I knocked on the door but no one answered. I checked my appointment book to make sure we had practice scheduled for 1pm that day, and sure enough, we did. However, it was obvious that no one was at the house, so I got back in my car for the hour drive home. I made a few more calls along the way, the first to Richard's cell phone, next the Williams' home phone, and finally Venus's cell phone.

Venus answered, "Hello."

"Venus, hey it's coach Dave. Are we practicing today?" I asked, already knowing the answer.

"Well, that would be hard unless you're here in New York. I'm going to play the U.S. Open," she said.

I knew it! Richard had not even bothered to tell me that he had decided to let Venus play the Open, let alone tell me practice was cancelled.

"Is your dad around? Can I talk to him?" I asked.

"Oh, he didn't come. He should be at the house though or on his cell phone," Venus replied.

"Ok, thanks Venus. Good luck! I think you're playing really well right now," I finished.

"Thank you, Dave."

I had not bothered to tell her that I had just been at the house and no one was around. It did not matter anyway because she had more important things to be thinking about. She was about to make her debut at the biggest tournament of all, the U.S. Open. The biggest that is, if you're an American. Good results at the U.S. Open would bring about a slew of sponsors, fans, and recognition.

Venus's best result so far was the quarterfinals at Indian Wells in March, not enough to call her year a success. However, the U.S. Open would change all of that. The 1997 U.S. Open will always be known for two things. First, it would be the grand opening of the new Arthur Ashe stadium. The word was that it promised to have the best comforts money could buy. Second, it was the year of the infamous bump between Venus and Irina Spirlea in the semifinals. The stadium speaks for itself and unless you are an architect there is not much else to say, except that it is beautiful. The bump however, now that was an exciting moment.

In Venus's first round match against Larisa Neiland she lost the first set 5-7 and in doing so, looked very nervous. Neiland had a good slice off both sides, which forced Venus to bend her knees even more to get down to the low slice bounce. This is not easy for a six foot one inch player. Venus was hitting too short, allowing Neiland to come to the net in that first set. Venus adjusted her game and then started overpowering Neiland, finding the rhythm of her ground strokes. She won the next two sets easily, 6-0, 6-1. She was now in the second round of her first U.S. Open.

The second round was Venus's easiest of the tournament. She won 6-0, 6-1 in just thirty-five minutes. That led up to the meeting with Anka Huber, who Venus had just lost to three weeks earlier. This time, Venus was ready for everything Huber had to offer. Venus was running down balls that even the crowd had given up on, and sometimes it surprised Huber so much that she would net the next shot. Huber was obviously feeling the pressure, because she had some key double faults and missed a lot of short balls. Venus won in straight sets 6-3, 6-4.

The media was getting excited. Venus had just beaten the eighth seed and had done it in convincing fashion. The post match press conference was packed with reporters from all across the globe wanting to know if the 'Cinderella of the ghetto' was going to make a run at the title. Next up for Venus was a doubles match with partner Serena, against Kathy Rinaldi and her partner Jill Hetherington. Venus had the edge on Kathy in singles, however, that edge was no help in doubles. Kathy and her partner showed the two teenagers that doubles is more about strategy than power. Venus and Serena went down swinging 6-4, 7-5.

The next day I talked with Kathy on the phone about the match. She said they were impressed with Serena's powerful returns and the way both girls played with no fear, but they just lacked doubles experience. In the doubles post match interview a reporter asked Venus what changes she had made in her game between the time she played Huber in Manhattan Beach and now. Her answer showed that she was strategizing much better in her matches. She said, "She was attacking my forehand, which was very weak at that time. So, I had to adjust that and just hit through it more like I regularly do."

Next in the draw was Joannette Kruger to be played on stadium court. Venus loved playing in the stadium with the big crowds. You would think that a sixteen year old, who did not play any big junior tournaments, would get nervous in the big arena, but not Venus. She loved to show off her stuff and the more people watching the better. Venus handled the twenty-three year old Kruger in straight sets, 6-2, 6-3.

After the match, Kruger said she had never seen such confidence in someone so young. She said she felt intimidated and got psyched out. She also claimed that Venus smiled rudely at her on a changeover. The media swarmed Venus about it in her press conference. They asked Venus if she was smiling rudely at Kruger. "No it was just an amused look," Venus said. She may have been amused that Kruger had no weapons with which to hurt her. Then a reporter asked her about an incident that had upset Lindsay Davenport. Davenport said she had smiled at her in the locker room and Venus had not smiled back. Venus's response was, "When I want to smile, I'll smile. If I don't want to, I'm not going to. I think it's a little bit peevish. Smiling. What does that have to do with anything?" Venus had a good point and in my opinion, it should not have even been an issue.

There was however, something of an issue building on the WTA tour. Underneath all the tennis that was being played, a wave of resentment and jealousy between the older players and the new teenage sensations had emerged. The teens showcased their athleticism, attitude, and sex appeal. Martina Hingis had already established her dominance by becoming number one at age sixteen and now Venus, who had been talked about for six years was starting to win. Behind them was Venus's sister Serena, the beautiful Kournikova, and Mirjana Lucic, who had won the first tournament she entered earlier in the year. All were poised and ready to take the places of the aging and ailing veteran players, who had occupied the top rankings for the past ten years. The older players were looking for respect from the teen sect, but the teens did not respect anyone but themselves. So all the articles written and magazine covers they adorned were simply expected marketing procedures promoting tomorrow's stars. The media had caught on and was watching closely, looking for more fuel to add to the fire. The WTA was happy with the notoriety that the tour was now getting. The women's game had become boring with Graf and Seles winning twenty-eight of the last thirty-six grand slam singles titles between 1988-1996. There was almost no airtime and fan interest was at an all time low. The emergence of this cluster of talented teenagers was a welcomed sight to the tour, and the WTA did their part in making a conscious decision to help promote tomorrow's stars today.

Venus was in the quarterfinals now and played Sandrine Testud. This was the furthest Venus had gotten in a pro tournament and her confidence was at an all time high. The first set was a back and forth baseline battle. Neither player was giving into the other's depth or pace. Finally, Venus was able to break Testud's serve and won the first set 7-5. The second set Venus got down two breaks and trailed 1-4. It looked like the old pattern was again surfacing. Nevertheless, Venus started changing the pace on her serve to get better placement and it seemed to throw off Testud's return game. With nerves biting, and the American crowd rallying behind Venus, Testud dropped serve twice, giving Venus a four game run to go up 5-4. Testud held serve and then Venus held, then at 6-5 Venus broke serve to win the match. It was a great comeback and it put Venus into uncharted territory. A semifinal.

In the media room, Venus talked about her newfound strategy of letting the other players make the mistakes, like it was something new that we had not been working on all year. Venus always had to absorb the information I gave her, toss it around for a while, and then figure out if it fit into her agenda. Once she made that decision, whether it was that day, a month, or years later, she then took credit for it herself. It helped her stay self-assured, I think.

"It used to be a time when other persons forced the mistake from me and I was not quite able to understand that I didn't have to go for winners, or I didn't have to always just expect to hit a winner," Venus said in response to a question on where she had figured out that she should mix it up. "I think I just started doing it in practice, mostly because Serena does it quite a lot. I think I learned it from her," she added.

Ever since she had been scolded for saying I was also her coach, at the Lipton Tournament earlier in the year, the only ones to get any credit for her success were Richard, Oracene, or the family. It did not bother me that she would not give me any credit, and I sometimes had to laugh at how obvious it was that she was avoiding to fully answer coaching questions from the media.

Another subject that surfaced at this time, a subject that would make world headlines a few years later, was what was going to happen when the sisters had to play each other.

"It is just going to be throat to throat, I guess," Venus was quoted. "We both have already discussed this and we said, you know, Serena says, 'I am going to take you out,' I say, 'Serena I am going to have to get you too,' so we definitely discussed it. We both are going to try to win when we play each other."

Since Serena was not playing much yet, the subject was dropped quickly. Later on, it wouldn't.

XIX

September 5th, 1997, was the day of 'the bump' and the day Venus lived up to the hype. Venus was playing Irina Spirlea in the semi-finals of the U.S. Open. She was unseeded and Spirlea was coming into the tournament having one of her best years ever. The animosity that was building between the older and younger players had Venus and Spirlea on opposite sides of the fence. Although Venus did not care to get involved, Spirlea was very vocal about the lack of respect shown by these new kids on the court. She took that feeling into the match and used it as motivation to try and beat Venus. The first set was a classic dogfight, going all the way to a tiebreaker. Venus was on the attack most of the set because Spirlea hit her a lot of short balls. Venus was able to capitalize on that and won the first set in a tiebreaker 7-6 (5).

Spirlea was obviously annoyed, and she showed it with facial expressions that looked like she had attended a Jim Carrey acting class. Instead of smiles though, there were lots of frowns and angry looks, all beamed in Venus's direction. For the fans, it made the match much more intense and more combative than usual, and for a New York crowd, that was the best type of match. The second set was as tight as the first. Spirlea was hitting her forehand deeper, now causing Venus to make more errors. Spirlea must have tried to drop shot Venus a dozen times, or at least it seemed that way, because Venus was scrambling to the net a lot. She got them all, as she had told her mom that day on the practice court she would. At 4-3 in the set, the players were changing sides of the net, as is always done after every seventh game.

As Venus and Spirlea were about to pass each other at the net, Spirlea moved in front of Venus causing a collision from both players. Venus was obviously concentrating and quickly held her hand up as if to say she was sorry and then preceded to her seat. Watching the match on television, everyone had a clear picture of Spirlea moving purposely to cause the collision. CBS kept the cameras rolling on Spirlea, and it showed her looking up at her coach right after the bump, smiling about what she had done. Normally that would have been an intimidating thing to a young player, but Venus was so into the match that she did not think anything of it. However, Venus did drop that set 4-6, which meant it was one set a piece, and now the winner of the third set would be going to their first ever grand slam final.

In the third game of the third set, Venus double faulted three times and faced break points. Her toss was getting blown around in the wind, and she was not being patient enough to re-toss the ball. But Spirlea made two unforced errors, and Venus held strong. That was the only let down Venus had in the set, and Spirlea did not take advantage of it, so the set went to a tiebreaker. Venus got down early in the tiebreaker 2-4. Spirlea looked as though she had things under control and went up 6-4, giving her two match points. I was sitting on the edge of my seat thinking, 'Please Venus be patient, be patient'. This was not the time to try and hit one of her thunder forehands. She erased one point and then came the shot of the tournament for Venus. After a few exchanges, Spirlea took a mid-court ball and hit an angle shot to the service line/sideline area. Venus was in the backcourt and the shot looked unreachable. But with two or three leaping steps, that reminded me of that first day I saw Venus hit at the Deerfield Beach Tennis Center, she covered the distance and hit a backhand that curved in from the outside of the court catching the sideline with about ten percent of the ball. One percent, ten percent, that's all you need. I've always told my players that a ball that's 99% out is 100% in. I was jumping up and down, screaming so loud that I scared my dog, McGyver, out of the room.

It was 6-6 and the players changed sides of the net. This time, Venus was paying attention to where Spirlea was as they crossed paths. This was all about guts now. Just the type of situation Jimmy Connors used to thrive on. Could Venus? It went to 7-7 and then destiny took over. Venus won the next two points and the match 7-6 (5), 4-6, 7-6 (7). She was in the finals. My phone started ringing almost immediately. Friends and family were all calling to congratulate me, and a few reporters were calling for comment. This was big time news.

Venus had the biggest press conference of her life. The media room was overflowing with reporters who wanted to know how she did it and if the bump was intentional? Venus was very diplomatic in her answers concerning the bump. She said, "I think we just both weren't looking. It's not really a big thing to me." Concerning the victory she said, "When I first won, it was like I was so happy because it was a long match we both worked so hard for it. Luckily I came out the winner." Venus's press conference answers were getting better. She was answering more from her heart now and not the pre-practiced answers she mostly used. The last question of the interview asked where she got her motivation. Venus said, "From God."

It looked as if the bump was going to be down played and not an issue in the tournament. At least that is what Venus wanted. CBS called Venus on for a live interview, in which she was ambushed by Pat O'Brien. He told Venus that Spirlea had said that she had done it purposely and said that Spirlea had used a cuss word in front of her name in the press conference. Then, on live TV, he asked her to comment. Venus was wide-eyed and obviously unprepared for this type of questioning, but she did as she had the whole tournament when under pressure, and delivered an eloquent response refusing to get drawn into a discussion of whether or not the bump was racially motivated. Now maybe the incident could be dropped, right? Wrong. Richard had already angrily commented to the associated press via phone, that Spirlea's actions were racially motivated and that Venus has experienced racism on the tour. These were some heavy allegations, which would be brought up time and time again.

The finals of the U.S. Open in 1997 looked like a junior U.S. Open being played on stadium court. Hingis, only sixteen years old, was coming into the finals without having lost a set in the whole tournament. Venus, who had just turned seventeen, was on the biggest roll of her career and coming off an emotional semifinal win. Venus's previous two matches against Hingis showed signs of greatness, but always came down to the fact that Hingis was more consistent. Venus's new found strategy of mixing up the pace of her shots in order to stay in the points longer was going to be put to the test against the steady minded Swiss star.

In the first set, Hingis showed Venus and everyone watching why she was the number one player in the world. She destroyed Venus 6-0. Venus helped a lot along the way with unforced error after unforced error. The first game of the match told the story of the entire first set. Venus was up 30-0, then 40-15 on her serve, but then committed four unforced errors, giving the game to Hingis. It was an early turning point in the match. Maybe nerves had something to do with it, since this was the biggest match of Venus's life. Nevertheless, Venus had always claimed that she did not get nervous, and to the press she had admitted that sometimes she just couldn't stop the errors from occurring.

In the second set, Hingis got the early break and led the set 4-3. Venus played a great game and broke back to tie the score 4-4. Then, on her serve, she went up 30-0. Two more points and she would have the game and a chance to break for the set. Hingis steadied herself though, and forced Venus into a few long rallies. Then Venus made a couple of unforced errors and the tables were turned. Now Hingis was up 5-4, serving for the match. Could Venus pull off another comeback like she had against Spirlea? Maybe she could, but the 'Swiss Miss' was not going to give her the chance. She served out the match, winning 6-0, 6-4.

Venus's breathtaking run at the U.S. Open title was over. The home-schooled and home-trained girl, who did not play junior tournaments, had come up one match short of fulfilling her destiny. The excitement of Venus, Hingis, and the other teen queens had the WTA breathing easier about the state of their game. The tour was heading into new highs as far as fan popularity was concerned. New rivalries were born and old rivalries were rekindled. It looked like sunny days ahead. But, there was one dark cloud lurking amongst all this enthusiasm, and it was created by Richard himself. His insinuations and accusations throughout the tournament suggested that the U.S. Open was rooted in racism. His proof was the infamous bump, Spirlea's words spoken in her press conference, and her obscene gesture, which Richard said was targeted at Venus. But at the same time as he was claiming racism, he also called Spirlea 'a big white turkey'.

Before playing the race card, one must know that Spirlea, one month earlier, ripped apart the tour's blond sensation, Anna Kournikova. Spirlea was obviously jealous of the attention the younger players were getting or just ignorant, but I would not call her racist. Players do not have to like each other, but they should all show each other a certain amount of respect. Until that happens, there will always be feelings getting hurt. The tour consists of players from over seventy-five countries, all representing different ethnic, cultural, and religious backgrounds. Some of these countries have been at war with each other for hundreds of years, but on the athletic field, the one thing that has been learned is tolerance and respect, to drop arms and compete.

Venus's press conference after the Hingis match should have been all about her great play during the tournament, but unfortunately, she would have to field questions about her father's comments.

Q: "Your father is quoted by the Associated Press as saying you have experienced racism on the tour. Could you comment on that?"

Venus: "I really, I don't think that's even part of it right now. I don't want to answer that question."

Q: Venus are you disagreeing with your father then?"

Venus: "I think with this moment in the first year in Arthur Ashe Stadium, it all represents everyone being together, everyone having a chance to play. So I think this is definitely ruining the mood, these questions about racism."

Q: "Your father didn't have to comment yesterday."

Venus: "You didn't have to bring it up."

Venus left the media room upset at the questioning. She had probably forgotten that she had even played a match, as the questions had gotten away from the tennis. At least she was done with press conferences for a while and could return home to the security and sanctity of the house in the woods.

XX

Venus's popularity was at an apex, and after the U.S. Open, she appeared on TV shows, did magazine covers, and conducted interviews with every media imaginable. We had two weeks of practice before she went off to Europe, and I had kept all her interview transcripts, because I wanted to show her what her own comments reflected as far as what she needed to work on in practice. The first day back was all hugs and congratulations and stories of the incredible run. We laughed about the Spirlea bumping, even going so far as to reenact it every time we made changeovers that day. It was pretty funny until we both knocked knees and fell to the ground, laughing in pain. Then on one of our breaks, we sat down and Venus got serious. There were a lot of comments made about her at the U.S. Open by some of the other players and that was on her mind. She asked me, "Do you think I'm as mean as they say I am?" I could tell that her feelings had been hurt by some of the comments. A few of the other players had called her everything from arrogant and cocky to insensitive and disrespectful. I had a simple answer for her. "They were jealous," I said. "You are new to the tour and you're getting lots of attention, so it makes them jealous. Try not to worry, you're cool." She nodded her head in thanks, but it was obviously still on her mind while we played sets. I knew, because I beat her 6-4, 6-0 in less than an hour. I told her not to worry, and that we would get a fresh start on Monday. She agreed.

Monday came, and I sat at the courts waiting for someone to appear from the house. After about an hour, I fell asleep listening to the wind blow through the pines that surrounded the Williams property. I awoke to one of the dogs licking at my bottle of Gatorade sticking out of my tennis bag. It was another no-show, and Richard was not answering his phone either. I returned the next day to find the house full of cameras and reporters from the television show 60 minutes. I did not have a chance to ask if we were practicing, because Morley Safer caught me at the front door.

"Are you Dave Rineberg? Do you mind if we interview you?"

"I don't mind," I said.

Then he asked me about ten minutes worth of questions. Serena grabbed me just as I finished and asked me to hit with her. Venus was going to be tied up for a while, so Serena and I went to the courts.

On Friday, People Magazine was out to do interviews with everyone. In between interviews, I hit with both Venus and Serena. During Serena's hit, she fell so hard going for a drop shot that she sprained her wrist. She was crying, and Venus took her inside to nurse her injury. Richard was doing his interview, so I walked over to listen. I had heard most of it before, but one of his comments really stood out. He said that Venus would make over a billion dollars in her tennis career. 'If that was the case,' I thought, 'then how come he owed me for the last three months?' I decided to hit him up for it when he was done. When I told him he had not paid me in three months, he seemed shocked. He immediately got on his cell phone and called into the house, which was just fifty yards away, got Venus on the phone and said, " Venus I want you to write out a check for five thousand dollars to Mr. Rinesburg and bring it out to me." Ten minutes later, I had a check in my hand and there were hugs going around from Richard and Venus, thanking me for my efforts. Everyone sure seemed happy, I know I was, and why not? 1997 had been a big year so far.

When Venus left, I asked Richard about the contract he had promised me since things were going so well. He gave me his typical song and dance about how he appreciated all my coaching and that he would have to have a family meeting first, then talk with his lawyers and okay it with them. In other words, it was not his decision.

The thing to know about Richard is that when he does not want to do something or he does not know how to do something, he always puts the blame or decision off on someone else. He only wants to take credit for the successes, not the failures. If he were to give me a contract, he would be saying to the world that I had helped in developing Venus and Serena's games, that in reality, he was not the great master coach that he had hyped himself up to be. So, to my face he continued to praise my efforts, but to put it down on paper and make it public knowledge was another issue, one that was never going to happen. I guess I knew that by then.

The rest of '97 was mostly played out across the Atlantic. In Filderstadt, Venus lost in the first round of qualifying. "Ouch!" is how she described it to me. In Zurich, she won all three rounds of qualifying and then got to the main draw quarterfinals where she lost to Lindsay Davenport 6-0, 6-4. In Moscow, she started in the main draw, got to the quarterfinals, and lost to Jana Novotna 7-5, 6-4. She came back to the United States for her final tournament of the year, held in Philadelphia. She took a wildcard into the main draw, and guess who she drew in the first round...Irina Spirlea. Richard had since apologized for his comments about Spirlea, but many things had been said since the U.S. Open, and a lot of issues had been raised. It was going to be interesting to see who handled it better, Venus or Spirlea.

Spirlea came out as if she had something to prove, maybe because she thought Venus had gotten a little lucky at the U.S. Open, or because she thought that she really was the better player. Whatever the reason, she beat Venus 6-3, 6-2. Venus seemed tired. Traveling to and from Europe had taken its toll on her, and she needed a break.

XXI

We had four weeks of practice time left and then 1997 would be over. Richard was into golf at this time and he had turned his acreage into a mini golf course by putting up golf flags in a few locations. His new thing was to hit a bucket of range balls at each flag while Venus, Serena, and I practiced.

Coach Rempel was out to play sets again with Serena this one particular day, and I was working with Venus on her forehand. As Rempel was making an approach shot and charging the net, from out of nowhere came a range ball that hit his side of the court skipped twice, and caught him on the anklebone. He let out a yell, "what the!" We all stopped playing and looked out across the field. Richard and one of his buddies were hitting our way. They were about one hundred fifty yards away, and the flag they were aiming for was twenty yards behind our courts. Richard must have put a good hook on the ball to get it to land on Rempel's court. After that, we couldn't help but flinch every time we heard a ball bang off the fences. Mrs. Williams, who had been sitting under the court canopy watching, got up and went inside the house where it was safe.

In our last practice before the holidays, I showed up at the house as usual, parked my car in the driveway, and walked across the field toward the courts. Richard was already out there, sitting in his golf cart smoking one of his brown cigarettes. I walked over to him for the usual greeting before proceeding to the courts. He was parked beside a group of palm trees that were growing out of some sort of knee high bush. As I got up to the cart, I noticed two things, one was a wine cooler and the other was a handgun, lying beside him on the golf cart seat.

"Is that real?" was the first thing I asked, in a rather startled voice.

"Sure it is. Do you want to shoot it?" he asked.

"No way man. I can't stand guns. I'm scared of them. I can't even pick it up. What are you doing with it?"

I was definitely nervous about the gun. Richard said he had a big black snake living in the bush beneath the palms. He said he had shot at it twice before and missed.

"But today I'm going to get 'em," he said.

Just then, Venus came out of the house and ran over to us. She asked her daddy what he was up to and he told her the snake story.

"I'm going to play sets today. Is that okay daddy?" she asked.

"Yes, Ms. Williams."

We started warming up, going through the usual crosscourt and down-the-line drills. Richard was walking around the bush, and I tried to keep one eye on him and the other eye on the ball. It did not work so well, I was framing more shots than an art gallery. Venus was up on me 3-0, when BANG! I hit the ground. Richard had fired the gun into the bush and I just lay there on the court for a few minutes. Venus was not even startled. She walked up to the net and asked me, "Are you alright?" I got up and walked under the court canopy. She followed.

"Venus, I can't play with that gun around. I'm sorry, I've just never been around guns and never really handled them," I said.

She looked at me and smiled, but I did not smile back. She knew I was not joking, because I smile at everything, so she went over and told her father that I could not practice with the gun around. He put the gun in the glove box of the golf cart and said he would wait until I left before he hunted down the black snake. However, it didn't help. The gun may have been out of sight, but I knew it was still there. I shook the whole practice and was never so relieved for a practice to be over. Richard promised not to bring the gun out during practice again. I thanked him and said I would see him next year. I was going home to Kansas for a peaceful and safe Christmas.

The roller coaster had ended the year at a peak. Venus had reached her own personal goal of breaking the top thirty with a year end ranking of twenty-two. The other highlights that made 1997 'the big year' were the following:

- Venus became the first woman, to reach the finals in her debut at the U.S. Open since Pam Shriver in 1978.
- She was the first unseeded female finalist at the U.S. Open since 1958.
- She was the lowest ranked woman to make a grand slam final since 1979.
- She received the WTA tours Most Impressive Newcomer Award.
- She was named the U.S. Olympic committee Female Athlete of the Month for September 1997.
- Tennis Magazine named her the 1997 most improved female pro.

SERENA
SURREAL

XXII

In the dictionary, a shadow is defined as 'a darkened silhouette cast upon a surface by a body intercepting the rays from a source of light, an imperfect and faint representation, an imitation of something, a copy'. To grow up in someone's shadow can be a cold, dark place. Many people said that Serena grew up in Venus's shadow and she definitely did. But being in someone's shadow can make a person stronger or wiser and in the end even better, if they have the will to break out of that shadow and become their own person.

I grew up with an older brother, a younger brother, and a younger sister, who all played sports as I did, and who are now successful in their careers. Nevertheless, I remember times in our childhood, when each one of us was in the shadow of another sibling. Since we all attended the same high school, it was impossible to get around without hearing about the Rineberg who had just graduated and all of his or her accomplishments.

My older brother, Rick, was a senior when I was a freshman. He was a four-sport letterman, who had a state basketball championship to his credit. If not for an almost paralyzing football injury, I have no doubt he would have gone on to have a great college football career as a quarterback. Since we lived thirty miles from the city and I could not drive, he was assigned the job of lugging me to and from school. He would have to take me to his basketball and baseball practices, or whichever sport he was currently playing. I sometimes got to play against the older players, which quickly helped me learn that if I was a factor in winning, I would get asked to play more, but if I lost, I would be given the task of water boy or scorekeeper to keep me on the sidelines and out of the way. I hated to be on the sidelines, so I practiced on my own to hone in on my skills in every sport. When the other kids were at the mall, I was working on my jump shot, curve ball, or serve. Why? Because I did not want to be just my brother's little shadow, I wanted to be my own player. All my hard work paid off, and it was that foundation that got me out of my brother's shadow and to where I am today.

The same was true when I was a senior and my little brother, Tom, was a freshman. Although I had raised the bar Rick had set, Tom was doing his best to break out of not only my shadow, but Rick's as well. Tom had twice as much adversity, which could have been too tall a task for him to even try to conquer. However, my brother broke through, and what came out of it all was the purest jump shot the family had ever seen. To this day, Tom can pick up a basketball and shoot from anywhere on the court, and with just the right amount of arch and backspin hit nothing but net.

Then it was little sister Charlotte's turn to go to high school. One might think she would just avoid the whole sports scene and take up cheerleading or some other activity in order to get out from under the mountainous shadow of her three older brothers. Instead, she looked at that mountain and, much like Lance Armstrong, destroyed it in every way possible, setting high school scoring records in basketball, winning the state tennis title in doubles all four years, and going on to receive All-American honors in doubles her freshman year at college! This led me to believe that being the youngest maybe had its advantages.

Serena was the youngest; in her case, the youngest of five girls. Venus dominantly cast the shadow Serena faced, because of her tennis profession, however, add in the success of the other sisters and the shadow Serena was in might have seemed like Mt. Everest!

In 1998, Serena and Venus began the year in Sydney, Australia. It was the first trip to Australia for both of them. Serena would be playing the qualifier, because her ranking at the time was just a little over one hundred. She had made her pro debut in 1997 and played in her first main draw at the Kremlin Cup, where she lost in the first round. In her second WTA main draw event, the Ameritech Cup in Chicago, she upset number seven, Mary Pierce, and number four, Monica Seles, on her way to the semifinals. She was the lowest ranked player (# 304) to ever defeat two top ten players in the same tournament. Those two wins catapulted her ranking and did wonders for her confidence. She had so much stored up power, aggression, and newfound confidence that I felt sorry for anyone in her path in 1998.

The first to fall in her path was Gloria Pizzichini, a player none of us knew anything about. However, Serena wasted no time getting to know her; she blew her off the court in straight sets 6-3, 6-1. Her next opponent was a talented player from Florida, Corina Morariu, who had proven results in singles, but was mainly known as a doubles player. Serena had a good fight on her hands, and the more intense the match got, the more aggressive and powerful Serena became. Morariu was trying to take away the sunlight that could break Serena out of Venus's shadow. Serena was not about to let her take it, and much like a child who was having something taken away from her, Serena struggled to hold on. She won the match 7-5, 6-4.

In her final round of qualifying Serena was up against another player none of us knew, but Serena dismantled her quickly 6-2, 6-0, showing an arsenal of shots that differed from Venus's power game. That win put Serena into the main draw, which alone would have been a great start to her first full year on tour, but Serena had waited too long to stop at the main draw. She wanted more and was ready for all that the tournament had to offer.

In her first main draw match, she was up against Mirjana Lucic, another tenacious teenager, who had qualified as well. Lucic had already proven herself on tour and was touted as the next great player by many of the European reporters. The great Steffi Graf had even given Lucic a plug after she played her, saying that out of all the teenage wonders Lucic could be the best. However, that was before Hingis's dominating year in 1997 and Venus's big late season run. The hype surrounding Lucic just seemed to fuel Serena.

Serena started out nervously, probably realizing the situation at hand, and lost the first set 6-4. Serena rallied and won the second set 6-3. At one set apiece, both players were swinging freely and attacking every ball as if it were their last. At 5-5 in the third set, Serena got the break and won the match 4-6, 6-3, 7-5. She jumped in excitement at having won. The sunlight had crept in, but Serena was not yet satisfied with the light.

Serena then went on to beat the seventh seeded Sandrine Testud, when Testud had to retire at 7-6, 3-0 down. This put her in a quarter-final match against a player that Venus had not been able to beat in all of 1996 and 1997, Lindsay Davenport, or 'The Big L' as Venus called her. Davenport showed Serena why she was seeded number two in the world, by winning the first set 6-1 in less than forty minutes. Serena had not even come close to breaking Davenport's serve and was making an unusually high amount of unforced errors. In the second set, Serena fought like a cornered dog with a bone. She cleaned up her strokes and started to move Davenport around the court, opening it up with short precise angles. Davenport was a power player, much like Venus, but she was not nearly as mobile. Serena's angles forced Davenport to do much more running than she was accustomed to and that wore her down, opening up the lines for Serena. Since Serena was not able to out-power hit her, she was going to have to out-hustle her. This was where Venus had always failed in her previous matches against Davenport. She had always entered into a slugfest with Davenport, who was much steadier and just plain better at that type of game than Venus. Serena ran down everything and won the second set 7-5. Davenport became frustrated at Serena's ability to sit back and counterpunch without making the unforced errors her sister Venus had always given up to her. She began to rush her serve and Serena was able to break. Serena then held serve to win the match.

Serena had accomplished something her big sister had never been able to do - she beat Davenport. She had clearly stepped out of Venus's shadow and into the direct sunlight for everyone to notice. And notice they did. The media frenzy began once again. Serena was in the semifinals of her first tournament of the year, and she was now playing one of the older generation players, former number one, Sanchez-Vicario. If Serena could pull off another upset, she would be in the finals and have wins over three top ten players, another great feat Venus had not yet accomplished. However, in the semifinal match Serena came out tight, and against the feisty, consistent Sanchez-Vicario that made for a quick match. Sanchez-Vicario won 6-2, 6-1, putting to rest any thoughts that Serena was going to win in her tournament debut at Sydney. But it was not just that Serena was tight, her game just did not match up against Sanchez-Vicario's, and they were too much alike. Both used their quickness and pinpoint placement of shots to pick apart and wear down their opponents. Until Serena's power game developed, she would continue to struggle against that type of player, especially ones with ten years of experience.

Venus, who was also playing in Sydney, finally beat the number one player, Martina Hingis, in the second round and then cruised into the finals to face Sanchez-Vicario. Unfortunately, she was not able to avenge her sister's loss, like she had when she beat Anne Miller a year ago at Indian Wells. At the end of that Indian Wells match, during the handshake, Venus said to Anne Miller, "That's for beating my sister!" So, the Williams sisters had made it to a semifinal and final round. Serena had been big news reaching the semifinals, Venus was even bigger news reaching the finals, but the idea of a Williams vs. Williams final had been the biggest news of all. Somewhere in Florida, Richard could be heard boasting, "I told you so."

XXIII

The Australian Open in Melbourne was the next tournament on the girls' schedule. Serena had added the colors of Australia to her beaded hairdo. She wore green, yellow, and white beads. Venus had started 1998 just as she had finished 1997, on a roll. Serena was gaining momentum and already had the girls in the locker rooms talking about her. Did you hear about Williams beating Davenport? Who Venus? No, her sister Serena. It was like the gossip of a celebrity break up. The news of a Williams who was meaner and hungrier than Venus was gaining speed, like a semi-truck going down hill. Serena and Venus did not discourage the rumor, in fact Serena liked it. In an interview, Serena was quoted, "I like to be tough with those girls when I get out there. I don't want them to think, 'hey, she's going to give me an easy time. I'm not going to have to work as hard'."

Serena's draw had her up against Spirlea in the first round. It was her chance to return the favor for Venus's dismantlement of Miller and beat up on Spirlea for the bump at the U.S. Open. The match went three sets, and Serena destroyed her 6-1 in the third, putting her into the second round of her first grand slam tournament, a feat that would only be tied by her sister.

Venus won her first round, which set up the match most fans were hoping for in Sydney, Venus vs. Serena. There had been a lot of speculation on whether the new Williams, Serena, could actually be the better player in the family.

Since they had not played each other very often, it was an awkward first set that went to Venus in a tiebreaker. For years, they had watched each other practice on adjacent courts back home and probably even wondered how much better the other one was getting, but as long as I had been around, they had never played a competitive match. Richard would never allow it. He kept the competitiveness that siblings can feel towards one another off the practice court, which is probably one reason the girls are so close now and still best friends. So, it was only natural that they were feeling each other out, so to speak, in that first set.

Venus settled the 'who is better' dispute, by winning the second set and the match 7-6, 6-1. After the match, they had the traditional handshake, which turned into a hug at the net. It was obvious that this was something the girls did not want to have to go through too often. But, of all Richard's outrageous announcements, the boast about his daughters being number one and two in the world was looking like the most believable statement to leave his lips in years.

After her loss to Venus, Serena announced that she would play German male player, Karsten Braasch in a match. Braasch was thirty and ranked number 226 in the world. Serena and Venus had both made boisterous, outlandish comments that they could beat players on the men's tour ranked as high as 200. They were serious. Braasch, after hearing Serena say, "I'm going to take him out," not only beat her 6-1, but also rubbed it in on changeovers by smoking cigarettes. He had also played a round of golf earlier that day and I heard that he had a few pints in him as well. However, this would not put to rest the girls' claim that they could compete on the men's tour, and more fireworks were yet to come. Neither of them had ever been able to beat me in our practices, and when I mentioned that to Venus she said, "That's just practice."

Venus's singles run ended in the quarterfinals with another loss to her nemesis, Lindsay Davenport, in another three-set slugfest. But, she was making another run in mixed doubles and reached the finals, where she and partner Justin Gimelstob won their first grand slam title. Gimelstob was a last minute decision by Venus and it proved to be a successful one. They teamed together the rest of the year, winning their second grand slam title at Roland Garros. It did not matter that mixed doubles was not looked upon with the same grandeur as singles or even doubles, because getting that first taste of winning, especially a major championship, was exactly what Venus needed to make her hungry for more. I could not wait for her and Serena to get back to Florida, so I could see the effects that their successes in Australia had had on their games.

A few days later, the girls were home in Florida. The usual week off after any kind of travel was now a ritual, and the girls normally used that time to catch up on homework and play with their dogs. But this time, Serena had only one thing on her mind; cars! Venus had gone through the same phase in 1997 and had settled on a light blue (her favorite color) Toyota four runner. Serena was more outgoing though, and Venus's conservative practical choice just would not do for her. No, there were car dealerships to visit and exotic, unpractical, glamorous cars waiting for a test drive. She settled with a 'tweetie-bird' yellow BMW convertible.

We had a few weeks of practice before both Venus and Serena would play in Oklahoma City, a city only two hours from my hometown of Wichita, Kansas. During those weeks, the girls joked about whether or not they should wear cowboy boots and hats when they played. They also teased me by asking if I could teach them how to walk bowlegged in between points, since I was fresh out of that area. Little did they know, that over the rainbow in the Midwest would be a place where dreams would come true.

Serena had been practicing much harder since her return from Australia. She was happy with her results down under in every event, except her mixed doubles. Serena played mixed doubles for the first time ever at the 1998 Australian Open. She partnered with a young Aussie, named Lleyton Hewitt. Hewitt was the new boy on the circuit from Australia and Serena was the new girl on the circuit from America. It sounded like a perfect match, but sometimes two players just do not play well as a team, and Hewitt/Williams lost early in the tournament. When Serena returned to practice in Florida, she told coach Dave Rempel and I about her mixed doubles partner Hewitt.

"He is terrible!" she said. "I could beat him! That will be the last time that I will ever play with him. He couldn't even hold service."

Serena was quite full of herself, and the loss would not go down as her fault. I had not really heard much of Hewitt at the time, so I made no comment. We would all know him later though, as the 2001 U.S.

Open champion. I wonder if Serena remembered her prediction of Hewitt?

Serena's path to the pros was a paved superhighway compared to Venus'. Venus had already broken down all the barriers, whether they were racial, social, critical, or economical. Venus had been the pioneer in the Williams family and had blazed a trail, creating a formula for success. All Serena had to do was follow the path that Venus had laid in front of her.

In the first two rounds in Oklahoma City, Serena played flawless tennis. Then, as though she had never touched a racquet in her life, she was blown off the court by a hot South African, Joannette Kruger, 6-1, 6-1. Serena commented to me later, "I don't know who that imposter was out there?"

Venus's run to the final in Oklahoma City also consisted of some near perfect tennis, including her first win ever over the big 'L'. That put her in the finals against Kruger, whose game was blossoming. But in the finals, Kruger quickly wilted under Venus's sun, giving Venus her first singles title of her career. To top things off, Venus and Serena won the doubles championship, becoming only the third pair of sisters to ever win a doubles title. When Venus and Serena returned to Florida, I told them, "See, it must be good luck hitting with a Kansas boy before playing in the Midwest." They just rolled their eyes at me and took their sides of the courts.

It was an explosive year for the Williams girls! Everywhere you turned, there were articles, magazine covers, and television interviews with one or both of the sisters. The girls were receiving more attention on the tour and in the Williams family than anyone else.

XXIV

The Lipton Championships in Key Biscayne is my favorite tournament outside the U.S. Open. The love affair started in 1989, when I moved to Florida and attended the event for the first time. Pro tennis was a ghost where I grew up, and for big time tennis you had to travel outside the state. Walking on to the tournament grounds and seeing my childhood heroes' names on the giant draw sheets and their actual faces up close, instead of on a television screen, made me feel a closeness to my sport that I had never felt before. In order to see as many players as possible, I watched thirty minutes of every match my first day. I got stuck at the Michael Pernfors/Yanick Noah match. It seemed as if every shot was in slow motion. That was the day I decided to relentlessly pursue my profession as a player's coach in order to be able to hit at the tournament sites and meet all the players I had imitated over and over again on my driveway growing up.

Serena and Venus were both playing so well that they did not want to change any of their routines. Richard informed me the day before the tournament (an early notification for him) that both Serena and Venus requested my services at the Lipton Tournament. This meant that I would need to be available for practice sessions on the off days at the tournament site, warm-up hits before each match, and match charting of each girl. If both girls made it to the semifinals, it meant a full ten days of around the clock work. Not to mention driving an hour to and from the tournament site each day. It sounded great to me, exactly what I had envisioned that day in 1989.

I met the girls each morning in the lobby of their hotel on Key Biscayne. I would get up around 5am in order to miss the Miami rush hour traffic, which could sometimes strand a motorist for hours in their cars, like metal coffins, on the outdated I-95 freeway. I could not afford that scenario, because Serena was an early riser. She liked to be the first one on the practice courts, scheduling 7:45 or 8am practice sessions. Venus would take the hour after Serena so both of them could get an early hit, have breakfast, and grab a shower before heading to the tournament site to check the daily schedule for any changes in match times, which always started at 11am. I would head to the coaches' locker room for a quick shower and then meet up with Venus and Serena in the players lounge to arrange warm-up hits before each of their matches.

The players' lounge was like a live TV soap opera, and when I or anyone else walked through the door, every head turned slightly to see who was coming onto the set. Players of all nationalities huddled around tables, at computer screens, or on cell phones gossiping about the latest tour romances and possible upsets happening on the outside courts. Since the Lipton was a combined event, it made the players' lounge even more exciting. Men and women hanging around together always created excitement. For example, if Kournikova was spotted talking to any male player, the rumors would start throughout the tennis center that she had a new romance for the week. The players' lounge could be a place for romances to start, a place of solitude, or a place where friendships were rekindled. There always seemed to be a popular spot within the players lounge, either a group of couches or a banquet table, where the more popular women or men seemed to hang out. Card games, jokes, and small talk were exchanged, like volleys on the court, and I could always expect to see players like Davenport, Fernandez or Raymond there, but I would never see the likes of Kournikova, Hingis, Venus or Serena.

I was a greenhorn to the players lounge that year and probably stood out like a freshman at a senior dance. I tried not to get caught staring at all the different scenarios that were being played out each day, but I could not help wanting to be a part of what was going on. I was not on the sidelines anymore, but I had to keep reminding myself that I was not working with the most popular girls on the tour either. I was reminded of that one day, when I sat on one of the couches reading the paper. A player next to me asked, in a very foreign accent, if I was through with the sports page. As I handed it his way, he saw my coach's badge.

"So, who are you coaching?"

"Venus and Serena Williams," I said, realizing that I did not have to say Williams by the look of disgust that came across his face after I had said Venus.

"Oh," he said in a disappointed tone and got up and walked away.

I guess I was guilty by association.

Venus and Serena kept to themselves whenever entering the players lounge. As eyes followed them through, neither of them gave the slightest hint of a glance in anyone's direction. They would pass right by me, as they walked like two models on a New York catwalk, searching out a spot to hang for an hour or so. The lower ranked players would point and whisper as they passed by, but I never saw anyone come right out and say hi or greet them in anyway. The whole media hype that the Williams sisters were standoffish and would not say hello was baloney, it works both ways, and I never saw anyone go out of their way to be nice to them.

Serena whipped through her first three rounds of the tournament without dropping a set. She dismantled Chladkova, Spirlea, and Paulus before suffering a one set hiccup in her win over Schnyder in the fourth round. She then shocked number one ranked Martina Hingis in the second set of the quarterfinal match, winning it 6-1, and jumping to a lead in the third set, having two match points, but in a tiebreaker Hingis dashed away any hopes of Serena winning. Serena was upset after the match and told me that she would win the next time they played each other. "I'll beat her," she said. She sounded like Jimmy Chitwood in the movie Hoosiers, when the game was on the line and there was only time for one shot and he said, "I'll make it!" Speaking to the media after the match, Serena was quick tempered and when asked about how she rallied so successfully from the baseline with Hingis, she answered, "A lot of people think that black people can't rally and just think they're athletes and can't think. As you can see, that's not true. I can rally. Venus can rally." That was the type of answer you would expect from Richard, not Serena. It was his 'us against them' influence showing.

However, Serena had made history during the tournament when she beat tenth ranked Spirlea in the second round. She became the fastest player to beat five top ten players on the WTA tour, doing it in only her sixteenth main draw singles match. This broke the previous record, which was held by Monica Seles, who in 1989 defeated her fifth career top ten opponent in her thirty-third main draw match.

Venus had been quietly moving through her side of the draw in pursuit of her first big title and her second of the year. Richard was anything but quiet, creating a circus-like environment around him in the stands by holding up wacky signs during the girls' changeovers. The signs read: "The Williams drink Lipton ice tea" and "I love my mother-in-law in Saginaw, Michigan." He had the camera crews suffering whiplash as they spun around on changeovers, trying to get a shot of each new sign he held up. When he was not in the stands, he was walking the grounds of the tournament, shaking hands and hugging people like a politician running for re-election. He could not sit and watch a whole match and asked me, as he left, to tell him if I noticed anything we needed the girls to work on. I would often share the player's box with Oracene, Lynn (Venus and Serena's sister), a representative of Reebok or another sporting goods company, an agent, and maybe a financial advisor or lawyer. The entourage was growing, and with each match won and with each dollar of prize money received, more and more vultures began circling.

Jim Tierney had brought a bus full of his tennis members from Deerfield to watch the matches at Key Biscayne. Venus and I were practicing on one of the outer courts, getting ready for her match against Hingis. Richard was supposed to be there, but was nowhere to be seen. Venus decided to call him to let him know where we were practicing. As I looked around the stands during her call, I noticed a bunch of people I knew, some fellow pros as well as the members from Jim's club. As we began hitting again, I heard, "Come on Rineberg!" and "Show her your stuff. Quit holding back!" Venus glanced a few times into the crowd. I smiled at the shouters, but then got back to the task at hand, getting Venus ready for Hingis. This was not a practice match at the house in the woods, this was a tournament practice. I needed to hit Venus shots that would get her grooved and feeling confident. As much as I may have wanted to show my stuff, I had a job to do.

Richard was talking with Jim Tierney through a hole in the fence from outside the tennis complex. Richard had somehow gotten outside one of the fenced off areas and was looking for a way back in when he saw Jim. They got to talking, as only Richard can, and Jim made the comment, "Richard I have to admit, you beat them all at their own game." Jim was referring to the agents and the promoters, the tennis bureaucrats, who controlled everything and everyone. Well, anyone who feeds Richard's ego is given the honor of hearing one of his entertaining, yet often fictional, stories of how he did it or what he was doing next. In this case, it was a story of why he carried a small piece of brick in his pocket wherever he went. Jim listened, as Richard told him of how he had stopped an attack by the Crips, the Bloods, and the Pierou back in California. Apparently he had come to the rescue of a Korean shop owner, who had shot a little African-American girl, and was now facing the rage of the gangs. Richard intervened, and stopped the violence by smashing a brick into a thousand pieces. He asked the gangs that they, this one time, keep the peace and told each gang member to take a piece of the smashed brick as a reminder of this day. After story time, Richard and Jim came to the court where Venus and I were hitting. I hit serves, while Richard stood behind Venus, encouraging her to step inside the baseline more.

"Dave," he hollered to me, "serve about 63mph like baby Hingis." Then he laughed and got Venus and I laughing too. We left the court to go back to the hotel.

Serena was in the lobby of the hotel when Venus and I walked in. She ran up to Venus and said she had to show her something. She pulled out some jewelry that she had just purchased in Miami. Venus was all excited and their teenage giddiness was glowing bright, as they tried on different bracelets and earrings. If there was one vice these two girls had, it was shopping for jewelry. They often joked about how they needed a twelve-step program for their addiction. They walked away giggling, saying they would be right back. I was left standing with one of the bodyguards, while the other one went with Venus and Serena. The tournament provided bodyguards to the top players to help get them through the massive crowds of autograph and picture seekers, as well as for general protection during the tournament. To me this was a welcomed perk, considering the threats I had received.

There was one bodyguard in particular that always seemed to get assigned to us. One night, Venus and I went out to practice at court B, which was located in the center of activity just off the food court area. Spectators always lined the fences to watch the pros practice, while munching on hot dogs, pizza, and various other fast food goodies. The word quickly spread throughout the grounds that Venus was on practice court B, and the crowd grew to at least four deep on each fence. Our bodyguard called for back up, as he could tell that getting off the court and back to the safety of the players' locker room would be difficult. If Venus stopped to sign one autograph, she would get mobbed by the crowd and could be stuck for hours. It was too late for that kind of hassle, since she was first on the next day and needed her rest.

While we waited for the backup guard, I was talking to Venus, about how I thought her desire to win was beginning to shine through, and how her opponents were intimidated by that desire. Our bodyguard was obviously listening to our conversation, because as our backup guard arrived and began to usher Venus through the crowd, he turned to me and handed me a piece of paper from inside his coat pocket and then turned back to catch up with the other guard and cover Venus from the back. I stuffed the paper in the side pocket of my tennis bag and followed him through the crowd.

Later, on my drive home, I was listening to a late night sports talk show program, the kind I would never tune into during the day, but for some reason it satisfied my mind's need for information, while I was driving though the darkness. Suddenly, I remembered the piece of paper the bodyguard had handed me earlier. I searched through my tennis bag, but could not find it. I pulled out two days worth of dirty laundry, racquets, notebooks, and a variety of sports equipment and food supplements. I had it all spread out inside my car, but couldn't locate the note. When packing my tennis bag, I was always thankful for those extra compartments and various pockets, but searching for small things like keys, socks, a wristband, or in this case, a piece of paper had me cursing the makers of my tennis bag and wishing for a much simpler design. I finally reached into the small side pocket that was virtually invisible and found the piece of paper. I unfolded what turned out to be a typed quote that read,

"Desire is the key to motivation, but it's the determination and commitment to an unrelenting pursuit of your goal - a commitment to excellence that will enable you to attain the success you seek."
Mario Andretti, racecar driver

It went perfectly with the motivational talk on desire I had had with Venus that night on practice court B.

The next day, Serena and I were going out to hit when I noticed our bodyguard was ushering out Hingis. As we passed each other, we made eye contact and he winked at me with just the hint of a smile on his face. I smiled and mouthed the words, "thank you." I showed the quote to the girls, but unlike me, they did not comprehend the effects or power of a good motivational quote. I placed the quote in my Lipton notebook for safekeeping and future reference.

Venus came out strong in her semifinal match against Hingis and won the first set 6-2. Serena and I sat in the player's box and cheered wildly as she hit laser like ground stokes past Hingis, controlling every point that first set. Hingis had seen it before, and she knew that slow and steady was how the tortoise beat the hare and that is how she had beaten Venus every time in the past. Hingis won the second set 7-5. Serena screamed at Venus in the third set, "Come on Venus!", and Venus must have heard her, because she played the third set with patience and power, winning it 6-2. Hingis looked slow and weak in front of the capacity crowd. On match point, the fans in the top rows chanted, "Venus, Venus!" This chant was pounding in the stands as everyone there sensed a new champion was emerging. A champion that was more like them. Not a country club princess who had everything a girl could ever want, growing up with the best coaches and the best equipment money could buy, but instead, a girl from the ghetto who had come from nothing and had nothing, who practiced on public courts that were covered in broken glass and used half deflated tennis balls and out-of-date tennis racquets. A champion like Venus was what tennis was waiting for, and in every public park across the nation new dreams were being dreamed. If it were Connors and McEnroe that were credited with bringing the blue collar class into the sport in the early 80's, then you have to credit Venus and Serena with bringing tennis into the inner cities and making it cool to play in the late 90's.

Venus's victim in the finals was Anna Kournikova, the other Florida prodigy from 1993, who was now in her first year on tour. She, like Serena, had had to wait to play full-time according to the new WTA age eligibility rule. Venus had not seen Kournikova since that day at the academy, when she had come over from the west coast to play a junior tournament. Venus dropped the first set to the young Russian Diva, but displaying a more all-court game and a deepened desire, she won the next two sets and only gave up one game in the third set. She danced her way to the net after match point. It was Venus's biggest tournament win of her career and she climbed the stands to the players box to share it with her family and friends. "When I win," Venus said afterwards, "everyone wins." In those days she was still quite humble on the inside, no matter what she showed on the outside. The loss brought out the brashness of Kournikova at her press conference, where she refused to give any credit to Venus and touted herself as the better player. "She didn't beat me, I lost," she said, "That means I'm better a little bit than her. I made all the mistakes, right? So that gives me some confidence that I could play better." Whatever Anna!

Venus took home $235,000, pushing her career earnings close to a million dollars ($916,573). However, that was insignificant compared to the news of her and Serena's new rankings. As a result of the championship, Venus was now a top ten player, putting her into that exclusive club for the first time.

Serena's assault on the rankings was raptorial. Ranked number forty at the beginning of the tournament, she defeated three top thirty players en route to her quarterfinal finish. Her ranking subsequently catapulted to number thirty, after being ranked number 304 in November of 1997. She had moved up 274 positions in just four months.

This start to 1998 had Venus and Serena on top of the "girl power movement" that had seized the nation at the time. Young girls all across the country were sassily singing along to Brittney Spears and the Spice Girls, while getting their hair beaded like the Williams sisters. Their popularity showed that young girls were capable of doing anything. The fact that these two sisters could carry the future of women's tennis on their shoulders had generated even more interest. There was also a great deal of speculation as to whether the Williams sisters would eventually dominate their sport, each alternating at the number one position.

After the Lipton tournament, we had a month to practice before the girls would make another trip across the Atlantic for the clay court season. Richard asked me for my notes from the tournament, since he had become accustomed to me submitting my notes and newsletters to either him or the girls. 'At least someone is reading them,' I thought. There was so much talk about which sister was better, that I took the opportunity to submit a report that gave all the strengths and weaknesses of each of the girls. I titled it 'The Lipton Report' and it was not the girls' favorite newsletter I had ever written, because, for the first time, I candidly discussed their weaknesses and compared each sister to the other. The first thing I outlined was the serve.

• The Serve - Venus has the power, but lacks control. When she hits it at 115 mph, she does not place it very well. There is a need for more depth on the second serve, which has too much slice and not enough kick, so it tends to sit up for the taking. Serena's serve is just the opposite. She places it well, especially out wide on the deuce side, but does not generate enough power. More knee bend is needed and taking the toss at a higher point would help as well. Both are double faulting during key times of a match, and Serena's serve is breaking down, more often looking a bit more nervous on big points.

This was an example of 'The Lipton Report' and they did not like my comments. Before, I had expressed my critiques much more gingerly, trying not to offend the girls, but this time it was just the facts. I felt that they were both getting old enough that a little healthy criticism should not bother them, but it did! They both tried to prove all my assessments false. Since, in the report, I had said that Serena covered the court better, Venus seemed to work harder on moving side to side. Since I had said that Venus was more intense and concentrated, Serena would give me the lowered eyebrow look on every serve, trying to look more intense. It was exactly the response I was looking for, and it proved to be my best coaching strategy yet. The girls were definitely susceptible to the, 'I bet you can't do it' coaching philosophy, which I have found works well on most young, bumptious athletes.

On April 20th, Venus and Serena wanted to play sets, so I brought out coach Dave Rempel to play Serena, while Venus and I rejuvenated our rivalry. It was a windy, humid day, which was to be expected at that time of year in Florida. The wind frustrated Venus and she tanked the practice as soon as Richard left the courts. We decided to use the rest of our practice time to watch Serena play Rempel. We sat under the court canopy, and I pulled a notebook out of my tennis bag to make some notes. Something caught Venus's eye.

"What's that?" she asked, looking at a list of names I had written on the back of my notebook.

"Oh, that's my list of players who I have indirect wins over," I said.

"Indirect wins?" What's that?" She looked over the list, which included names like: Capriati, Rubin, Majoli, Huber, Spirlea, and more recently, Hingis, Davenport, Mauresmo, and Kournikova.

"You see Venus, an indirect win, simply put, is anyone you have beaten I have beaten too, because I have beaten you. I have beaten them through you," I explained.

"Serena!" Venus screamed, stopping Serena's practice. "Come here, you've got to hear this. Dave explain that to her." I went through the whole explanation again. Serena was wide-eyed as she hung on Venus's shoulder.

"See, I even have a column for you Serena." I showed her the list of names. "You've given me some indirect wins that Venus hasn't been able to get for me yet."

After Serena and Venus stopped laughing at me, Serena said, "You've got to write an article on that for us to use in our newsletter. Okay?"

"What newsletter?"

Venus and Serena had begun publishing their own newsletter about the happenings on the tour, which they called 'Monthly Tennis Recap.' They had printed up several copies during the Lipton tournament and left them lying around the players lounge. It included match results, player interviews and stories about the editors, which were of course them. They planned massive distribution at the grand slams, and a person could even get on a mailing list for future issues. They had given me my first deadline. They needed my indirect wins article before leaving for Europe in two weeks.

"Okay," I said, "but you guys have to get me some big indirect wins that are missing on my list, like Graf, Sanchez-Vicario, Seles, and Novotna."

"Okay," Serena said. "No problem."

Our last few days of practice in May were all about serves and return of serves. If there was one shot that most of the players feared from Venus and Serena, it was their return of serves. Why? Because, while most players are content with just getting the ball back in play, Venus and Serena had been taught to go for outright winners. To step inside the baseline and move forward towards the service line in order to take the ball on the rise and catch their opponents off guard. One of the drills we often did in practice highlighted the return game. They would try to return my fastest serves as I stood serving from the service line, instead of the baseline, where the serve is supposed to be delivered. They had both become fearless in their returns. A weaker serve delivered from the baseline must have looked like it was in slow motion, like a pretty little bunny, hopping over the net, compared to my service line serves.

On the red clay courts of Europe, where the ball slows down as it hits the soft clay, there would be ample opportunities to step up inside the baseline and take advantage of even the best of the women's serves.

On the flipside, for Venus and Serena, serving placement was going to be important. The slow clay courts would take away a lot of their power. Serena shined in this area. She had developed a keen angle slice serve to the deuce service box that had set her up for countless cross-court down-the-line combinations in her previous matches. She was now working on that same angle to the add court, but with more of a kick spin. The kick spin serve makes the ball jump high away from your opponents' power zone, making for weak returns in the center of the court, and anything hit into the center of the court was ravaged upon by Serena.

The tour moved into what is known as the clay court season. I really thought Serena would have more success than Venus, because her consistency off the ground toggled together with her speed was a better weapon than Venus's power. She also seemed more patient and was hungry for that first title. Venus, I thought, might suffer a let down, now that she had won a few tournaments.

The first stop was Rome, and Venus proved me wrong in her first outing. She made it to the finals, where she lost to Hingis 6-3, 2-6, 6-3. Along the way though, she gave me an indirect win over a player that I did not have on my list yet, Sanchez-Vicario.

Serena got to the quarterfinals, where she again lost to big sister Venus in straight sets, 6-4, 6-2. She had three good wins however, beating Conchita Martinez, Joannette Kruger and Natalia Tauziat.

The sisters had proven themselves on the red clay, and the French Open committee had taken notice. They purposely placed Venus and Serena on opposite sides of the draw, hoping for the all Williams final that had been talked about by the media and hyped by their father. Richard declared that he would not travel to any tournaments that did not place Venus and Serena on opposite sides of the draw, and he also said that he would not let his girls play the same tournaments anymore after this year. He claimed that since his two girls were going to dominate the tour, certain tournaments were placing them on the same side of the draw, to ensure that one Williams would be knocked out of the tournament before the finals.

It was an absurd statement, based only on speculation, but Richard used it to cry foul and also played the race card, trying to bully the tournaments into setting up their draws his way and not by lottery, which was used in most cases. He was a master at manipulating people, and unfortunately he used his daughters' careers to beat the system. If tournament directors and WTA officials did not adhere to his suggestions, he would not allow his daughters to play those tournaments. Venus and Serena were such huge attractions that no tournament director or WTA official would have wanted to miss out on the Williams sisters being in their tournaments. It was almost blackmail, and although I liked how he had orchestrated the girls careers up till then and had defied the odds by choosing the road less traveled, I did not agree with how he was now using their success for his gain. He had come right out and told me that his reasons for wanting them on opposite sides of every draw were so that they would have a chance of going farther in the tournaments and collect more prize money and more ranking points. All of which meant a fatter wallet for him.

XXV

One day in late June, Richard called me out to the house in the woods for a meeting. The girls were still in Europe. The tour had moved into its grass court season and Venus and Serena were now playing at Wimbledon. Richard had said that he wanted to discuss the details of a contract. I actually thought that because of how well Venus and Serena were playing and how much a part of their success I had become, Richard was finally going to offer me a full-time, three year coaching contract based on a percentage of the prize money earned and bonus incentives galore, as he had always promised. I imagined this meeting would be short, only needing my signature to finalize it into action.

When I arrived, Richard was out in the field next to the tennis courts, hitting golf balls into the pond about one hundred yards away. Parked next to him was a new Lexus SUV with a big poster print of Venus and Serena on the side rear panel. As I walked out to meet Richard, I could hear the stereo from the Lexus blaring out some hip-hop/rap style music. As I got closer, the lyrics caught my attention,

"Two girls from the ghetto, laying low," yada, yada, yada, something, something.

"Mr. Rinesburg, how you feel today?" Richard said, with a cigarette in one hand and a five iron in the other, as he gave me his usual hug greeting.

"I'm fine Richard," I answered in a curious tone.

"Do you like my music?"

"It's alright. Not my taste, but alright," I answered, knowing he was headed somewhere with that question.

"Listen to this next song," he said, as he reached in and turned up the volume even louder. This time I clearly heard Venus and Serena's names mentioned in the lyrics of one verse and the "master king Richard" in another.

"Okay, what's this?" I asked.

"That's my band and that's me doing the rapping on the chorus," he said with a grin that stretched from ear to ear. It looked as though he thought he had just produced a hit record.

"We're going to release it first in China."

'Oh no,' I thought to myself, 'here we go with the China stuff again'.

"Then we're going to hit Europe and last the U.S. market," he said.

He had apparently been working on this project since the girls were nine and ten years old, and famous rappers, whose names I did not recognize, had offered him millions for his lyrics. After an hour, I finally had to interject.

"Hey Richard, you wanted to talk to me about a contract or something?" I said.

He turned down the stereo, a little annoyed that I had cut into his bragging session. Just then, his phone rang. He answered it. It was Venus calling from Europe.

"Yes Venus. Okay, good Venus. I'll go watch. I love you." He then hung up. "Dave we will have to continue this conversation when Venus and Serena get back from Wimbledon. I need to discuss it more with the family."

He gave me a hug and got into the Lexus SUV and left. I stood in the field beside the house, looking into the setting sun and wondered what had happened to the meeting. 'Finish what? What had we discussed? Anything?' I looked down and saw the five iron and half of a bucket of golf balls. I picked up the five iron and proceeded to hit the rest of the golf balls into the pond. In my head, I tried to figure out the reason

Richard had called me out to the house in the first place. The only thing I could come up with was that he was lonely and just wanted the company of someone who would listen to his stories without passing judgment. That was me. I had been playing the role of listener, as well as the invisible coach, for more than five years now. Staying in the backdrop, out of the spotlight, and keeping my coaching on the practice court and out of the media. If there had been an academy award on the line for the best impersonation of a phantom or an apparition, then I would have won hands down.

Serena's quarterfinal result in Rome, along with her fourth round result at the French Open, had moved her ranking into the top twenty for the first time in her career. If she could have a good run at Wimbledon, she would crack the top fifteen faster than any women before her. Her second round match at Wimbledon was against Mirjana Lucic and was touted as a big test for Serena. The British tabloids picked Lucic to be the better grass court player. Serena took that prediction as an insult and used it to railroad Lucic 6-3, 6-0 in less than an hour. She was in the third round and it looked like she had a legitimate shot at reaching the semifinals in her first Wimbledon. This was another key win in a grand slam and it added to her persona, making her even more threatening. But her train was derailed when, against Virginia Ruano-Pascual, she fell and suffered a calf strain while trailing 7-5, 4-1. She had to retire from the match, which halted her bid at winning the women's singles crown.

Serena was not done at Wimbledon though. She had partnered with Russian Max Mirnyi in mixed doubles and they were making a run at the title. They were a very young team. Mirnyi had just begun to get his singles ranking up and he was very excited to have Serena as his partner. I remember he was so shy that his father was the one who had to set up the partnership. Mirnyi was a hard worker, but had one annoying habit in doubles: he loved to slap high fives after every point. Even on the points they lost, he would go right up to Serena for a hand slap and a face-to-face chat. I gave Serena grief about the constant hand slapping that was going on in their matches, because I knew she didn't like it. Serena would rather toss a racquet, pout, or stare down an opponent after playing a bad point, but Mirnyi never gave her a chance. As soon as the point was over, there he was, right in her face.

I would laugh at the occasional annoyed look on her Serena's face as Mirnyi walked away from the hand slap. Their youth made them a perfect match though. Neither wanted to disappoint the other, so they played hard and fought for every point. Most did not consider them a threat for the title because they had no experience, but in my opinion, that is exactly why they were a threat. They wouldn't fall victim to the pressure of the tournament. They quieted any doubters as to their ability, when they made it into the finals. Then, as if they had been playing together for years, they saved their best tennis for last and secured the mixed doubles title over Bhupathi and Lucic, who had defeated sister Venus and Gimelstob in the semifinals. Serena had her first grand slam title.

The sisters had now won the first three mixed doubles titles of the year, with just one more to go at the U.S. Open. A win there, would make it a Williams sisters' grand slam, winning all four majors in one calendar year. "I am the first Williams sister to win a Wimbledon title," the victorious Serena said. "It feels great." Serena was the first Williams sister to do a lot of things. If you compared Serena's first year on tour to Venus's, you would see that Serena accomplished much more. The only thing missing was reaching the finals of a grand slam in singles. She would have only one chance left, the U.S. Open in August.

Once back on the practice court, Serena had one goal in mind. She wanted to become a better volleyer. It was clearly a weak spot in her game, which was magnified in her mixed doubles matches. "All the men volley so well and the women, well, most stay back at the baseline," she told me before we began hitting. She wanted to hit crisp, penetrating volleys, and she wanted to do it as a serve and volley player. She had no fear of coming in to the net off the baseline, so it was just a matter of hitting a lot of mid-court transition volleys that were missing from her game. She was a baseliner who did not venture into that zone too often. After a few days of work, she was ready to try her new serve and volley game in a match.

Venus was hitting again, after taking a week off after Wimbledon, and so out to the house came coach Rempel to play Serena. I think Serena figured that if she said that she was now a serve and volley player, it would just happen and she would be successful. Well, Rempel, had a good return and proceeded to pass Serena left and right, winning the first set easily. After yet another mid-court volley error, Serena got so upset that she smashed her racquet deep into the clay court. The racquet was unusable after that, and when she went to her bag to grab another, she found that all her other racquets had broken strings. She got even more upset, so she grabbed her bag and exited the courts. Serena was intense and it didn't surprise me anymore when she walked off the court or smashed a racquet. However, Rempel had not seen it much, and he wanted a souvenir to remember the event. He took the smashed racquet and later hung it above his office door at the Deerfield Tennis Center.

Meanwhile, Richard was on court with Venus, trying to demonstrate how he wanted her to hit her return. Rempel, who now had no one to hit with, was watching as I hit serves to Richard. He had a cigarette sticking out of his mouth, no socks on, and his shoes weren't laced. I served one easy to his backhand. He swung at it so hard that the cigarette flew out of his mouth and he stumbled out of one shoe. Rempel busted up laughing on the sideline, which caused me to laugh and provoked a smile from Venus. When Richard got back in his shoes, he handed Venus her racquet and said that she had practiced enough for the day and that he needed to talk with Rempel and me.

Venus left the courts and went inside to check on Serena. I walked over, still chuckling a little bit at his demonstration, and even Richard laughed a little as he tried to light a new cigarette.

"Dave do you know a good court maintenance man?" was his first question to me.

"Sure," I answered. "A man I work with from Deerfield Beach is the best court guy you'll find."

"What's his name?" he asked.

"Eddie Gillion," I said, "Why?"

"I don't have time to take care of these courts anymore. I'm getting ready to start my own bus company," he said. "If you could write down his name and number, I'd like to contact him."

I wrote down Eddie's name and number and handed it to Richard. He then pulled Rempel off to the side and told him how much he appreciated him coming to hit on such short notice. He said that he was going to pay him a bonus of $5,000 for his efforts after the U.S. Open. Then he asked Rempel to excuse him, as he wanted to talk to me in private. Richard put his arm around me.

"I have discussed it with Venus and Serena, and I'm going to pay you a $20,000 bonus this year. Now, on top of that, I have worked out a sponsorship deal with BMW Motors for the girls. They are each going to be driving a BMW by the end of the week, and I got one coming for you as well."

"One what?" I asked.

"A BMW of your choice," he said. We began walking towards my car where Rempel was standing, waiting to leave.

"You got a BMW for me!" I said in an excited, yet curious tone.

"We'll work out the contract later," he said. "I'm also going to need you in New York for the U.S. Open. We have you a room booked at the Days Inn. And here's your plane ticket."

He reached into his back pocket and pulled out a folded up plane ticket to New York. This was a real ticket! He was not fibbing this time! Maybe the BMW contract was true as well. I was really pumped up. By this time, we had walked over near where Rempel was standing.

"Wow Richard, that's great! You're a pretty good agent," I said, complementing him on his generosity and deal making skills.

"Well you're a pretty good white boy," he said and then he laughed, gave me a hug, and drove away in his golf cart. Rempel had busted out laughing again and I said, "Did you just hear that?"

"Yeah, you're a pretty good white boy," Rempel said, as the tears of laughter swelled up in his eyes.

"So what was that all about?" Rempel asked, as we got in my car and began our drive back to Deerfield. I told Rempel of the bonus and the U.S. Open plane ticket, which he agreed were both expected parts of the job. Then I told him that by next week I would be driving a new BMW of my choice, as Richard had signed a deal with BMW and I was included in the contract. Rempel looked at me and I at him and then at the same time, we both said, "Right!", using our best sarcastic voices. Rempel knew all the previous promises Richard had made to me, which had not come true, and I explained to him that Richard was just trying to show off. "Don't think for a second that I'm still that naive," I said. I only gave the perception that I was still naive and gullible. That's why Rempel could joke about our promised bonuses even though I knew deep down he was hoping his would come true.

XXVI

Serena finished 1998 by winning a few awards. She received the WTA's Most Impressive Newcomer award, which was won by Venus in 1997, and the Tennis Magazine/Rolex Rookie of the Year award. It was a nice welcome to the tour, but without any singles titles, Serena felt incomplete. With her ranking high enough to get her into every main draw, she set out in 1999 in search of one thing, titles.

Paris is where Serena conquered her demons and won her first WTA singles title. She beat a talented player, Amelie Mauresmo, who was playing some of her best tennis at the time. While Serena was celebrating, half way around globe in Oklahoma City, Venus was defending her title, beating Amanda Coetzer. This marked the first time in WTA history that two sisters had both won singles titles in the same week.

Serena did not stop there though. She went to Indian Wells the next week and beat the second, sixth and twelfth seeds en route to the finals. There, she faced Steffi Graf, who currently had a finals winning streak of twenty. The two split sets, and Serena was down 1-2 in the third set, when she called for a trainer to treat a sore knee. This was never a good sign in my experiences with Serena. It usually meant that she was feeling inferior and that she was either stalling or trying to break Graf's momentum by taking a break. Either way, it did not help, and she got down 4-2, usually too far down to comeback against a champion like Graf. She broke Graf the very next game and then held serve. Serena took charge of the match from there on and closed out the set, 7-5.

Serena skipped across the court like Dorothy skipping down the yellow brick road. She hugged her daddy and Venus, who were there supporting her. Serena was asked about the win, which was her second in a row.

"This is the biggest tournament I've ever won," she said. "I know that I can win the big ones now." The victory moved Serena to number seventeen in the rankings. She had started the tournament at the twenty-first spot. She became the lowest ranked player ever to win a tier 1 event since the tier structure began in 1980.

You could call Serena butter because she was on a roll. She got to the finals the next week at the Lipton, but lost to older sister Venus and then she took some time off because of a knee problem. She missed the whole grass court season, but the time off had a positive effect. In August, playing at Manhattan Beach, her first tournament in two months, she won her third title of the year. She was in perfect form going into the U.S. Open.

What Serena did at the 1999 U.S. Open was unfathomable. She was seeded seventh and no seed that low had ever won the women's title in the Open era, since 1968. But no one told Serena that, and so she capped off an unbelievable year by winning the women's singles title. She had beaten big sister Venus to the ultimate achievement in the sport of tennis, and she did it in high fashion. She had upset number one, Martina Hingis, in the finals, number two, Lindsay Davenport, in the semifinals, and number four, Monica Seles. Serena became the second African-American woman ever to win a grand slam singles title since Althea Gibsen did it in 1958. Serena was the sixth American woman in the Open era to win the title, and her ranking moved to a career high, number four in the world. What else was there to do in 1999 for Serena? She had won a grand slam singles title, she had moved her ranking into the top four in the world, she had wins over four previous number one players, and she had won two grand slam doubles titles. Surely she had accomplished all she desired. But there was still one thing she wanted that she had not yet been able to do, beat big sister Venus.

Since Richard had decided to try to avoid entering the girls in the same tournaments, a decision he made at the beginning of the year, Serena's chances to defeat her big sister were limited. The Grand Slam Cup, a tournament played in Munich, boasts a purse of $6,700,000 to attract the best men and women players in the world. The winners of each event received over a million dollars in prize money, a carrot neither Venus nor Serena could resist. They both played the tournament, and since they were on opposite sides of the draw, the only chance of meeting would be in the finals. They were both playing the best tennis of their careers, and it did not surprise me that the finals were exactly where they both ended up. Serena would have her chance to beat her sister, and either way, the Williams camp would be taking home over 1.5 million dollars.

Serena came out and smoked Venus 6-1 in the first set. Maybe as the reining U.S. Open champion she expected Venus to roll over and die. Big sister came right back though, and won the second set 6-3. It would be one set for the million dollars, winner take all. Serena did not care that much about the money, and maybe that is what allowed her to raise her level of play in the third set and win the match. For the first time ever, she had defeated her sister Venus 6-1, 3-6, 6-3.

Her champion's smile seemed bigger. Maybe this victory meant more than anything else in 1999. Future successes would just be icing on, what had grown throughout the year to become a very large cake.

TOUR
STORIES

XXVII

The 1998 U.S. Open was full of high expectations for the Williams family. Both Venus and Serena were playing well and full of confidence. Richard, Oracene, and I were all making the trip to New York, which marked the first time all three of us were attending a grand slam tournament together. There would be plenty of coaching. Also attending was an entourage of people employed by the Williams' to take care of all loose ends. Venus and Serena had nothing to worry about.

I was in charge of practices and warm-up hits for the two-week period. I had never been in New York for more than four days at a time and was still insecure about how to get around the big city. Therefore, I decided to call one of my best friends from my hometown in Wichita, Kansas, Pat Egan, to see if he wanted to come and hang out in New York City and attend the U.S. Open tournament.

Pat had been forced into tennis in high school by being my friend. I often used him for serving practice or baseline ground stroke drills when I couldn't find anyone else to hit with me. Pat developed some good topspin, and over the years, our hitting sessions improved. Today our hitting sessions are full of good rallies, but don't ask Pat to stand at the net and just feed balls from a basket, oh no! That is not a wise thing to do. His big western forehand grip gave all his feeds extreme topspin, which either sent them into the net or landed them so short that the ball wouldn't even reach the baseline. Put Pat at the baseline and he was much more helpful.

Pat was glad to get my call and said that he would catch the next flight out of Wichita, Kansas and meet me at the airport. When Pat arrived, we grabbed a cab and headed straight to Flushing Meadows, where the U.S. Open is played every year, to pick up the credentials needed to get us into the behind-the-scene areas of the tournament. Pat's passion for tennis had grown since those days in high school when I had forced him to play. He had even gone on to coach his local high school tennis team, which had given him a deeper appreciation for the game. The U.S. Open had always been the tournament he enjoyed the most, so I knew that having the credentials to roam freely around the grounds and behind the scenes would be a huge thrill for him. Security was tight though, and it was not as easy as I thought it would be.

My name, which should have been submitted by my player, Venus or Serena, was absent from the credentials list. So even I couldn't get credentials until I first found Venus or Serena. Luckily, I knew that Venus was giving a clinic for Reebok, at 45th and Broadway, so Pat and I went off to find her. We took the number seven train to 42nd street and then ran over to the clinic at 45th. I found both Venus and Serena there and arranged to meet Serena back at the tournament site later that day to pick up credentials. However, when we arrived back at the tournament, I found that the Williams' allotment for guest passes was out and all that was left for Pat were a few day tickets. That just would not do, so Pat had to do a little Kansas finagling, and by the next day, he had a pass that would allow him to get in with me to the players lounge and everywhere else at the U.S. Open.

Pat was like me when I had gotten my first set of credentials. He would be sitting in the players lounge and excitedly lean over and say, "Dude, there's Agassi! And over there! Is that Kournikova?" I had to laugh at the Kansas boy in him, because I was the same way just a few years earlier. This was only my second U.S. Open, so I was still intrigued by the whole scene myself, but I now knew how to blend in so I didn't stand out like a tourist. Pat would learn how to blend in before he left, and would even end up having lunch at the same table as a few of the star players.

Having Pat there at the '98 U.S. Open was important, because I now had someone to give witness to all my friends and family back in Kansas. He could testify to the true circus and excitement that surrounded the Williams family. Venus and Serena greeted Pat with the usual annoyed, disinterested and rude looks that they greeted most every stranger with. It was only because Pat was a friend of mine that they even said hello to him. I was hoping it would not bother him, but the first thing he said when they walked away was,

"Are they always so rude?"

"They just have their guard up extra, because it's a big tournament. Don't mind them," I said.

"I couldn't deal with that attitude," he added. He went back to watch the practice courts, and I went to watch Serena's first round match.

Venus cruised in her first round match, while Serena struggled. Serena had not yet learned how to keep her emotions in check in critical situations, and after tanking the second set, she faced one of those moments at 3-4 in the third set. She got tight and played a few very bad shots. I could see in her eyes that she was about to let her emotions out. If Nicole Pratt, her opponent, would not have made a few quick errors herself, Serena would have lost control. However, Pratt could not see in Serena's eyes what I had learned over the years to be a dead give away; Serena was ready to quit. Pratt gave back the momentum and Serena won the match.

Serena was not as confident as she had seemed the week before the U.S. Open and it looked like she was doubting herself a lot in that first round. In my notebook, I wrote down a comment or two on every game. The last thing I wrote was, 'don't doubt yourself!' When Serena read through the notes the next morning, she pointed to my comment and asked,

"Could you see that?"

"I've been on court with you for the last three years, and I think I can read you pretty well now," I answered.

She raised her eyebrows and handed me back my notes. "Thanks for the notes," she said. Then we started practicing, trying to work on getting her confident again.

Venus came out to practice for her next round, and we had just started hitting crosscourt forehands, when Richard arrived. As soon as he walked on the court, I could tell something weird was going on. He was carrying a cardboard box full of tennis balls along with a racquet that had two broken strings. He was stumbling, as he walked, like the bums I had seen on Broadway the night before. His speech was slurred as he tried to bark orders at Venus on the opposite side of the court. He motioned me to take the net position next to him. As he fed a ball, he lost his balance and crashed into me. I was able to catch him before he fell to the ground, and one of the agents, who was picking up balls, came over and together we helped Richard to the courtside chair. "Are you alright?" I asked. However, what he said in response neither I nor anyone else could understand. At this point, Venus came over and had a worried look on her face.

"Daddy are you okay?" she asked, but he did not even seem to hear her.

The agent said that he would take care of Richard, and that I should go ahead and get Venus ready for her upcoming match.

After Richard was helped off the court, Venus and I started to hit again but Venus was rattled. I did not see Richard the rest of the tournament and not one person in the Williams family was talking. I was told, months later, from Richard himself that he had almost died. He said that he had flown straight from New York to L.A. to get emergency treatment. For what? I didn't even ask. If he wanted to tell me, he would.

That night Pat and I got back to the hotel pretty late. We were both tired from the day, but in New York that is no excuse not to go out. So we hit the streets of Times Square and the neon lights seemed to energize me as we walked down Broadway. The tourists filled the sidewalks, with cameras in hand, walking steadily, enjoying the sights. I was hungry, but Pat was still tired. I suggested going to a restaurant, he suggested take out. I suggested people and atmosphere; he suggested solitude and a comfortable bed. Therefore, we flipped a coin and I won. The next restaurant we found was a place called Carmine's on 44th street and Broadway. We popped inside for a quick bite to eat. The place was a throw back to the fifties style restaurant. The inside had pictures of old movie stars on the walls, waiters in all white, and the food was all served family style. The place was packed and everyone seemed to be enjoying themselves. We took a seat at the bar so we could watch the U.S. Open highlights on the TV. We ordered, and when the trays of food came, we found out what family style meant. We had enough food for three families and barely put a dent in each tray. I told Venus and Serena about it the next morning and invited the whole family to meet me there for dinner. They cordially declined. Socializing with anyone outside the family was never an option.

In the third round, Venus played Larisa Neiland. We were not expecting a tough match, but we weren't expecting Neiland to retire at 5-0 in the first set either. She had apparently injured herself pretty bad in her previous match and probably should not have even walked onto the court with Venus. After the handshake, Venus came off the court feeling cheated. She wanted to play. I suggested to her that we go to the practice courts and duke it out. She smiled wide, obviously confident about how she was playing. I went to get a practice court and all that was available was court number five. Practice courts were all the same I figured, so I grabbed two cans of balls and told Venus I would meet her on court number five. I had to go get my racquets from the coaches' locker room, which was located in the old complex. We normally practiced on practice courts one through four, which were all lumped together and fenced off, so the players who wanted to avoid the rambunctious U.S. Open crowds could practice in some sort of privacy. I felt very comfortable there, and so did Venus.

As I hurried across the grounds towards the practice courts, I noticed a large crowd forming in the stands and around the fences of a court where I had watched Sampras practice earlier that morning.

"Could you tell me where practice court five is?" I asked one of the U.S. Open attendants.

"Court number five is right there," he said, pointing to the court with the large crowd.

I walked over, and through the crowd I saw Venus stretching out at the net. The crowd was already eight deep and I almost got into a fist fight with some New Yorker, who said I was full of it when I told him I needed to get through to hit with Venus. Venus was all business as I stepped on the court. She said she was already warm and that as soon as I warmed-up we would play a set. We began hitting ground strokes from the baseline, but to me it felt like we were on opposite ends of a football field. I could not believe the crowd that had swarmed around the court to see Venus practice. Some people had seen this as an opportunity to see the number six seed play without buying a ticket to the stadium court, where she usually played her matches. Others had had a ticket to her match with Neiland and had not had a chance to see enough of her since Neiland had retired early. Whatever the reason, all I know was the word must have spread throughout the U.S. Open grounds, because people were coming from everywhere!

I was suddenly feeling the electricity that was being generated by this U.S. Open crowd. For years, I had heard Jimmy Connors say that he fed off of the energy of the New York crowds, but I was not Connors, and the effect on me was going in the opposite direction. My racquet began to feel as if it weighed a hundred pounds, my feet felt as if I were standing in quicksand, and my eyesight was fading in and out of blurry and blurrier. I was going down fast! I was not ready for this kind of pressure. I had played in front of crowds bigger than this in college, but this was the U.S. Open crowd, which over the years my mind had turned into the Godzilla of all crowds. I motioned Venus to meet me at the net for a conference. I think she could tell that I was nervous by my last three shots, one of which I hit off the frame and into the tenth row of the stands.

"Venus, this crowds is huge!" I said. "I have to tell you I haven't played in front of a crowd this size in quite a while. I'm feeling a little tight. I'm not going to be able to give you a good hit."

"I play in front of this kind of crowd all the time," she said. "I love it!"

For a minute, I didn't think she was going to let me off the hook, but then she said, "I guess if you're not used to it. Anyway, I don't need to hit. I feel good. Let's hit in the morning."

"Thanks, I owe you one," I said, and we began to exit the court. However, Venus started to sign autographs, so we did not get off court number five for another thirty minutes! There were even a few kids who ran up to me and asked me for my autograph. That sure made me feel better, even though they probably thought I was the famous pro tennis player Richey Reneberg and not Venus's coach, Dave Rineberg.

Through the rest of the tournament we practiced on practice courts one through four, or the stadium court. The stadium court was awesome for two reasons. One, the crowd of on-lookers could not get below the second level, so they were unnoticeable to us while we were playing. Second, it was the U.S. Open Stadium Court, the court that the finals of the U.S. Open are played on each year. The same court that all the great players over the years have played on, and the same court where Venus and Serena would one day hold the U.S. Open trophy high above their heads.

Kathy Rinaldi was at the U.S. Open that year, doing commentary for USA Networks. I tracked her down, since she had told me to stop by the USA booth while I was at the tournament. She was scheduled to commentate one of the matches on the outside courts and was heading over to see the make-up artist when I found her. She asked me to go with her so we could chat. On our way into the studio, we ran into Tracy Austin who was going to be commentating Serena's second round match, which was next on stadium court. Kathy and Tracy were friends from their days on the tour, and it was a real treat for me to be talking with these two great tennis legends. Kathy introduced me to

Tracy as Venus and Serena's hitting coach, as well as her coach from a year earlier. Tracy had a few minutes before Serena's match began and asked if she could ask me a few questions. She wanted to get the inside scoop on how Serena was playing. I obliged her with as much information as she asked for, and she obliged me by giving me a plug on national television during Serena's match. During the match she said, "I had a chance to talk with Serena's hitting coach, Dave Rineberg, earlier today...." I did not even get to hear or see it because I was in the player's box watching Serena's match with Oracene and Venus, but all my friends and family from Deerfield Beach, Florida to Wichita, Kansas heard it. Those people knew how hard I had worked and were happy to hear me finally get some credit for my coaching.

Serena won her second round match 6-2, 6-1. So, after a first round scare and an easy second round, Serena was into the third round of her first U.S. Open. Up next, was Venus's dance partner in the bump from a year earlier, Irina Spirlea. It was a close match that went three sets. Spirlea won the first set 6-3. Serena came back strong, and she must have been a little angry, because she didn't let Spirlea have a game that set, beating her 6-0. Serena had a good third set record for the year (7-3) and she had beaten Spirlea once already, so I thought she had the edge going into the third set. However, Spirlea's experience pulled her through and she won the set and the match 6-3, 0-6, 7-5.

Serena was out of the singles, but still alive in the mixed doubles with her Wimbledon partner and the notorious hand-slapper, Max Mirnyi. She had planned to play with someone else, but after she and Max had won Wimbledon, Serena was quoted as saying, "I want to go for another grand slam title with Max." It was a good choice.

My duties as hitting coach were now cut in half, since Serena was out of the singles. She could get her warm-ups with her mixed doubles partner Max, and if she still needed more, she could hit with Venus at her practices. I continued to take the 7am train to Flushing Meadows each morning, although Serena wasn't practicing, to avoid the mad rush of people hurrying to their places of employment or in search of a morning coffee and bagel. I had found the rush began around 7:45am in the city. Since Venus liked the 9am practice time, and not the 8am that Serena liked, I had an extra hour to kill each morning.

In the early morning hours, I found the U.S. Open grounds to be a quiet, peaceful place. The stadium seemed like a church cathedral as it stood, empty of people, yet full in spirit. With the morning sun low on the horizon, the shadow cast by the upper stands darkened the entire west grounds and practice court area. It was nothing like the craziness that would web the grounds just a few hours later. I have always enjoyed the stillness of the morning for as long as I can remember. While some people wake in hopes of finding companionship, I wake in hopes of finding solitude, much like Henry David Thoreau who said, "There is no companion more companionable than solitude." I would grab a newspaper and coffee and sit out by court number five, which was my big choke court, to read the media's predictions for the upcoming day's matches. I really enjoyed listening to the morning music played throughout the grounds as I read my paper. Whoever controlled the music that year must have loved Sade, because each morning, at precisely 8am, the song *Jezebel* followed by the rest of Sade's greatest hits would play over the sound system and float throughout the empty stands of the silent courts. I became an instant fan; her voice seemed to blend perfectly with the sunrise and the cool air of the early morning. In my notebook I wrote a note to self, 'pick up Sade album after the tournament'.

Venus's first real test came in the fourth round against Mary Pierce. Venus served well in the first set and gave Pierce a lot of serves into the body, which she knew Pierce did not like. Add in the fact that Venus was hitting good deep shots and Pierce was making tons of errors, it was a quick first set for Venus, winning 6-1. The second set presented the real test for Venus. Pierce became aggressive and drew Venus into a slugfest. This caused Venus to deviate from her game plan, which was to be patient, move Pierce around the court, and wear her down.

The set went to 5-5, and there must have been nine deuce points before Pierce, in the eleventh game, finally made an error to give Venus the game. With Venus up 6-5, all she had to do was serve out the game to win the match, but that is sometimes easier said than done, especially when your playing one of the top seeds at the U.S. Open. After quickly getting down in that game, Venus hit a forehand long and just like that, they were in a second set tiebreaker. Venus was down 1-4, as Pierce had stepped up her game. I thought we were heading into a third set, but Venus won three quick points and hit one of her running down-the-line backhands, right on the line, to go up 5-4. She then backed that up with an ace and closed out the match. She jumped for joy at her mini comeback in the tiebreaker, winning that set and the match. The win put Venus in the quarterfinals against Arantxa Sanchez-Vicario.

XXVIII

Venus was into the second week of the U.S. Open and that was the week George Bezecny came up to New York. He had some friends (players) he had come to see, and I told him that he could stay with me and use Pat's credentials for access to the tournament, since Pat had gone back to Kansas.

I got back to my hotel to find that George had just arrived in the city. He was watching the Cardinal baseball game when I entered the room, and Big Mac was stepping up to bat. This was the year that Mark McGuire and Sammy Sosa were competing to brake the home run record. We said our hellos and then both stared at the television. As McGuire came to the plate, the tension grew, and it seemed as if all of New York was quietly watching. McGuire had 61 home runs and one more would break the record. The count built and finally, Big Mac saw a pitch he liked and sent it out of the park! The announcers went crazy and so did we. They must have shown the replay twenty times, and the announcer's screaming voice blared out of the TV, "Remember where you are folks on this memorable occasion, because this feat may never happen again!" I will always remember George and I watching it happen in our hotel room at the 1998 U.S. Open.

The next morning at practice, I asked Venus and Serena if they had seen Mark McGuire's record-setting home run, but they showed no interest, and when I asked them who they wanted to end the season with the most home run hits, Serena spoke up first.

"Sammy Sosa definitely."

"Yeah, I don't want that McGuire guy to win," Venus added. She and Serena both liked how Sammy showed the crowd he loved them with his heart pat and peace kiss after every home run.

"Serena, maybe you should do that in your future mixed doubles matches after Max's hand slap," I said as I laughed. She just glared at me. The girls loved to make fun of me, but they couldn't take it when I made fun of them.

The night of the Sanchez-Vicario/Venus match it was cold and windy. Venus struggled with the conditions along with Sanchez-Vicario's game. She lost the first set in typical fashion, by making a ton of errors. Then, as if someone had turned on a light switch, she lit up the stadium with her blinding display of the new power game that was overtaking the tour and leaving the veterans, like Sanchez-Vicario, behind with their control games. She blew out Sanchez-Vicario in the next two sets, winning the match 2-6, 6-1, 6-1. After the match, I gave Venus my summary of notes on how she had played during the match. They were as follows:

- First set you didn't stick to your game plan.
- You broke down her forehand by being so consistent.
- Tonight you learned how to set up a point and restart a point.
- Need to work on second serve placement.
- Don't spot your opponent any games.
- Be consistent from the start.
- Your power game is too much for the older players.

It was late when Venus got out of the media room, and I was planning on hitching a ride with her back to the city, but somehow I missed her. I knew that I now had to catch the number seven train that goes from Flushing Meadows into the city, which I had been riding each morning for the past ten days. However, I had never ridden it this late at night, because I usually got a ride from someone or hopped on the player's bus. I got on the train with my tennis bag over my shoulder, and took a seat near the middle of one of the cars. I was surprised at the number of people on the train that late at night, but then again, this was New York, the city that never sleeps. About half way to the city, at one of the stops, a group of guys got on my train car. They seemed to stare at me for a few stops, and I was thinking about all the New York cop shows that I had seen, portraying the subway as a place of crime and murder. I started to get a little paranoid, which probably triggered what happened next. I had my head down the whole time, acting uninterested in what the guys were doing. I was therefore unaware that they had moved and were now sitting directly across from me. Just then, out of nowhere, my nose started bleeding like crazy. I quickly pulled a white towel from my bag to soak up the bright red blood. You should have seen those guys split. I mean they almost tripped over each other, getting off at the next stop. I had my face buried in my towel and was laughing at what had just happened. I guess if I had seen some guy start bleeding all over the place, I am sure I would have run too. At least now, I knew how to clear out a train car in New York City.

I told Venus and Serena about it the next morning, and they rolled on the ground with laughter. The more I thought about it, the more I laughed too. I always used my stories as a way of keeping the girls loose. They were into real life drama.

Venus played Davenport in the semifinals, and it was an emotional match for her. She had already lost control a couple of times this year. Once, at the Australian Open, in a match against Davenport, she was penalized a point for losing a row of beads from her hair for the second time. Venus screamed at the umpire while holding back the tears. Second, at Wimbledon, in a match against Jana Novatna, when a call went against her during a crucial moment in the match, she almost cried and again yelled at the umpire that the call was not fair. Venus's game has always ridden the wave of her emotions. When she was happy, her game was on cruise control, but when she was upset, her game was more like a car crash. In the first set, at 4-4, her facial expression and her body language told me the tale. On the outside she began over-hitting, which is what she would do when she felt out of control on the inside. At 4-5, she made four errors to lose the first set. She needed to calm down, but her emotions were controlling her game now, and she couldn't get settled. At 3-3 in the second set, she finally exploded emotionally and made three quick errors. Her forehand had gotten tight and she didn't have any fight left. She was just free swinging at the ball, which caused more errors than winners. She ended the match on an error and ended her chances of repeating last year's incredible run to the finals. This time though, her tournament run was a concentrated effort, with planning and purpose, as opposed to the fated miracle run of 1997. In that regard, this tournament served more purpose in Venus's development as a player and as a person.

Serena came out of her first U.S. Open with the mixed doubles crown, making it a Williams grand slam in the mixed doubles events of 1998. Venus and her partner Justin Gimelstob had won the Australian Open and French Open titles, and Serena and her partner Max Mirnyi had won Wimbledon and the U.S. Open titles. All four in one year for the Williams family was quite a treat and another feather to add to their caps.

At the 1998 U.S. Open, it was hard for me to stay out of the spotlight as I had done in the past. With Richard's mysterious absence, the media was looking for the person who was pulling all the strings. Choreographing the practices was easy compared to dodging questions that might get me in hot water. I always remembered a scene from the movie Bull Durham about doing interviews. Kevin Costner was helping the team's pitcher with his interviews for his major league debut. 'Keep it really boring and stay humble' was the point Costner was trying to make, because nobody, especially other players, likes to hear someone blowing their own horn. If I knew the reporter, or they came across sincere, I would give them a lot more information than I would the pushy kind.

The college tennis team from Bethel, Kansas was attending the 1998 U.S. Open. Bethel was in the same conference as my college, Friends University, and I knew their coach from our team battles and the Kansas summer circuit, where we had both played every year. At a practice during the Open, while Venus and I practiced on practice court four, I kept hearing someone yell, "Hey Dave!" from behind me, behind the windscreen. I waited until Venus needed a break before I began to scan the back fence to see who was calling my name. I recognized a familiar face and walked over to the screen.

"Hey Dave, remember me?"

"Sure, Marty, how are you?" I responded. We visited a little while, and he told me that he had his tennis team with him and none of the guys believed that he knew the guy who was hitting with the Williams sisters.

"Would an autographed ball be proof enough?" I asked.

"Sure!"

Venus and Serena were both on the court, and I don't remember just whose signature I got for him, but as we exited into an area where the public could not go, I tossed him an official U.S. Open practice ball with the signature of one of the Williams girls. He was delighted; he now had some proof for the Kansans.

I found that the autographed tennis ball from either Venus or Serena was a popular request from all my tennis students. Before I had left to go to New York, I must have had thirty requests for autographs from my junior academy kids. I could not promise them anything; Venus and Serena were touchy about signing anything, even for me. Therefore, what I did over the two-week period of the 1998 U.S. Open was to get one or two autographs from the girls at the end of every practice session. By the end of the tournament, I had forty-four balls, twelve ticket stubs, and three draw sheets with their autographs. About forty of those were Venus's, since she had more practice because she had stayed in the tournament longer than Serena.

It had become such a habit for the girls to sign a ball for me after practice that when we got back to Florida, at the end of our first practice, Venus held out her hand to me while I was packing up my bag. I did not know what she was doing, so I reached out and shook it.

"Nice practice," I said with a puzzled look.

"Don't you want me to sign something?" she asked. I laughed, but seized the opportunity. I pulled a ball out of my pocket, and she signed a quick Venus across it. Then she handed it back to me, smiling. I think she understood why I had laughed. Venus's signature had changed from the early days in 1993-1994. She used to sign her entire name, dot her i's, and try to be neat. However, after signing thousands of autographs between 1994-1998, her signature had shortened to her first name only with a star above the 's' in Venus. She could scribble ten quick Venus's in the time it used to take her to write out one neat 'Venus Williams'. Don't tell me that she had not learned a thing or two on tour.

XXIX

The Swisscom Challenge, a tournament in Zurich, Switzerland, marked another final for Venus in 1998, and another loss to Lindsay Davenport. Nevertheless, tennis fans will always remember that tournament because it was there that Venus Ebony Star Williams broke the world record for the fastest women's serve of all-time on the WTA tour.

It happened in her quarterfinal match against Mary Pierce. Venus was having a relatively easy time with Pierce, having won the first set 6-4, she was up 5-1 in the second set and serving for the match. Pierce looked as if she had thrown in the towel because Venus was playing too strong that day. On match point, Venus, doing her best impersonation of Pete Sampras, rocked back and fired a 127mph (205 km) ace to win the match. The crowd clapped for her victory, as that is the usual courtesy, and then, noticing the record speed of the serve, roared into applause. Venus had shattered the old record, held by Brenda Schultz McCarthy, of 123 mph. This was not a fluke either; Venus had been knocking on the door all year long, hitting a 122 mph serve in Miami and a 120 mph serve at Roland Garros. Venus was ecstatic! She finally had the confidence in her serve that had been lacking all year. When she returned to practice she told me, "If I can hit a serve like that, then there's nothing else I can't do!" I did not understand where she was going with that statement until a few weeks later.

On November 23rd, I found out precisely what she meant. Venus had come to practice with one thing on her mind, change the forehand. Most players would have looked back at the year Venus had just had and been quite satisfied. Not Venus. She was looking to improve and she was maturing enough to understand that change was sometimes a good thing. Venus had a western forehand grip, which had a tendency to break down on her from time to time. Some of her worst losses occurred, because of the absence of her forehand during the match. Players would pick on it fiercely. That day at practice, she told me, "I want to hit my forehand more like Serena. She has a more eastern forehand." I think she had not only been watching Serena's forehand, but also Hingis's and Davenport's. She had lost to them countless times over the past two years, and they also hit with a more eastern forehand grip than her. Richard and I discussed the change and concluded that it would be a good move. I stood at the net with a basket of balls and fed one at a time to her forehand side as if I was teaching a beginner. Her first twenty shots went over the fence behind me, like a Sammy Sosa homerun, and with each one came a laugh or a scream from Venus. I am sure she had not felt so incapable in years. The rest of the day was more of the same, and at the end of practice, Venus had a sore wrist and my side hurt from laughing at all the jokes she and Serena kept cracking as balls flew over fences, hit light poles, and ricocheted off water coolers. I suggested to Richard some drills that would help Venus make the change, but he insisted on letting Venus work it out for herself. "I'm not always going to be there for her, so she needs to learn on her own," he said. Each day it was more basket feeds to the forehand and slowly, but surely, the balls started to come back down to earth. A slight adjustment to semi-western and Venus was now able to hit the ball inside the lines again.

A week later, we began to rally from the baseline at moderate speeds, and it was apparent that Venus was handling low balls much better, which was one of the main reasons for the change. There was still the occasional ball over the fence when she pulled up as opposed to hitting through the ball, but she was making progress. I actually thought that after a week, she would be back to her old grip where she felt comfortable, but she was determined to make the change. After one month, she had made the change successfully and the only balls causing her problems were high bouncers out wide. Her grip had settled more into a semi-western, but she did occasionally go into a full eastern. I was amazed at how quickly she had made the change and it showed me that she was also learning something about self-discipline. With just two weeks left before the 1999 season, Venus was now working on trying to take every ball on the rise, but she still hadn't got the timing down on the new grip.

I asked Venus, "What do you think about the forehand change? Are you ready?"

"This is going to help me win Wimbledon, right?" she asked. "So, I'm sticking to it."

'Wow, did this girl have a vision or what?' I thought to myself. I now had no doubt that she would be ready for 1999.

Venus had a superb year going into the 1999 Lipton Championship. She had defended her title in Oklahoma City, she had reached the quarterfinals at the Australian Open in Melbourne, and made it to the finals in Hanover. In my opinion, there was only one other person on tour playing as well, and that was Serena. Going into the 1999 Lipton Championship, Serena had won her two previous tournaments with wins over Hingis, Davenport, and Graf. Some said she was the hottest player on tour. Therefore, it did not surprise me when both girls made it into the semifinals at the Lipton. On Venus's side of the draw was Steffi Graf. Venus had just beaten Graf in Hanover in a tough three setter. In our practice before the match, Venus was very confident in how she was hitting her ground strokes, so we concentrated mostly on the serve, which was powerful but still somewhat of a scud-missile, not always falling in the intended area of the service box. Richard did not like how she was tossing the ball and made her toss about fifty balls into a cardboard box. He loved to use a cardboard box in practices, he said it let people know he was from the ghetto. Venus had a tendency to hang on to the ball too long, which pulled the ball over her head instead of being out in front of her. We were practicing late that night at Venus's hotel on Key Biscayne. When we came off the court, there was a camera crew waiting at the steps of the entrance to the hotel. It was a Spanish station that wanted a comment from Venus. Usually, Richard would not allow such an intrusion, but he was in a good mood and allowed a quick interview. When Venus finished her interview and walked into the hotel, the camera turned onto me and the reporter asked me for comment. He would ask me a question in English and then interpret my answers in Spanish. Venus and Serena were very popular in South America, the reporter told me, "This footage is going straight to South America for tonight's news," he said. I figured that this made it safe to do, because Richard was still not happy with an interview that I had done in January with the Boca Raton News, a local paper with very little distribution. The title of the article was, *Rineberg Coaches Williams' Hitting*, giving notice that there was someone else, besides Richard, coaching the girls. He was even quoted in the article as saying, "Dave has been with us a long time. He's genuine and just a great guy." I thought that was a great compliment, giving me the green light to speak up more often in the future. However, Richard's moods changed like the ocean tides, and he had already come down on me for showing my match notes to Venus, one morning at practice. As always, I took notes of the girls' matches, writing down swing flaws, strategy mistakes, and situations good and bad. I was showing Venus my latest notes, when Richard walked over and asked what I was doing.

"I'm showing Venus my notes from the last match," I said.

"Well, don't show your notes to Venus or Serena ever again, I don't want you confusing them," he said, with a horrible look on his face and a nasty tone in his voice. I had been showing my notes to the girls for the past four years, but now, for some unknown reason, he did not like it, so I had to stop.

Serena played Hingis in her semifinal match. Serena had not played Hingis at all that year, but she had seen Venus play her plenty of times in the last two years. Serena knew that she had to hit with depth, in order to open up the angles. Richard wanted Serena to run Hingis side to side because, he said, her legs were too short to keep up with Serena.

I thought he was just saying that to Serena to get his point across, but later I read the quote in a newspaper article. It wasn't my choice of strategy. You can beat ninety percent of the women on tour by hitting deep, pushing them back, and then going wide, running them side-to-side, but up and back also.

Venus handled Graf in straight sets 6-2, 6-4. The win put her into the finals for the second year straight. This was a title she needed to defend to maintain her ranking. However, Serena had a much tougher fight on her hands with Hingis. Serena won the first set 6-4, but struggled to a tiebreaker in the second set. Serena was trying to avenge a quarter-final loss to Hingis on this same court a year ago, where she let two match points slip away. This time, there would be no mental lapses. Serena played a gutsy tiebreaker, fending off all of Hingis's tactical moves to try and push the match into a third set and won the match in straight sets 6-4, 7-6. The win set up another all Williams match. However, unlike the previous all Williams match in Munich, this was a final of a Tier 1 event, with ranking points on the line, mainly Venus's ranking points. Venus had to defend her points from winning the Lipton in 1998 if she expected to stay at the number two position in the world rankings.

Serena had bettered her results from a year ago by reaching the finals and seemed to be ready to win her third straight tournament of the year, especially since she had beaten Venus in their last meeting at the Grand Slam Cup. At least that is what the media thought, but I knew better. Serena would not like to hear this, but in my opinion, Venus will beat her nine times out of every ten times they play. It is not just that Venus is better, it's more the fact that Serena has always looked up to Venus and at times even idolized her. When they were younger and went to a restaurant to eat, Oracene told me stories about how Serena would wait until Venus ordered and then order the same thing. Venus used to walk Serena to school and as they approached a busy street they had to cross, Serena would not go without first reaching for Venus's hand. Venus was her protector, her defender, and sometimes her idol. How could Serena go about beating her? It would be the same as me trying to beat Jimmy Connors, whom I idolized growing up. If I got up a break, or say even a set, I would think, 'no way am I up a set on Jimbo! He must have given that set to me', and then I would probably doubt myself right into defeat.

On the flip side, Venus would not beat Serena ten out of ten times either, because, Serena was the little sister that she had protected, consoled, and sympathized with all her life. She would have to give her baby sis a break every once in a while and let her win. I saw her do it in practices for five years, and I think she already did it in Munich.

The girls did their best to act as if their matches against each other were like any other matches, but it was apparent to me, and many others, that their matches were not of the same quality. When practicing before playing Hingis or Graf, Venus and Serena were so focused. They would hit every ball at me or past me as if I was their opponent. Sometimes I would stop and say, "save it for the match Venus," or "don't waste it on the practice court, Serena."

Practice the morning before their Lipton final was what I liked to call a, 'hit and giggle' practice. Serena would switch to her left hand when Venus was about to serve the ball to her, so Venus would then play the next ten minutes left-handed, laughing all the way. "I want to see you do that in the match," I said, as I stood at the net tossing them balls. When Richard came out to the courts, the laughter was gone, and Venus and Serena got serious. They did a few drills while Richard yelled out commands, switching them in and out of hitting against me. He kept them hitting separately just like he had done all those years out at the house in the woods. First, Venus would hit ten shots as hard as she could in the opposite direction of where I was standing, then, Serena would jump in and swing away, trying to hit a winner on every shot. I was standing with my hands on my knees after twenty minutes of trying to retrieve all those shots. But that is how every practice and warm-up had always been. There's no way Venus and Serena could practice with any of the other girls on the tour. They would be the worst practice partners in the world, because they wouldn't let their practice partner work on their game. When tour players practice together, they normally hit shots to each other to get some feel going, then hit to specific court locations and maybe play some points. However, Venus and Serena would never hit the ball right back to someone. When they see open court, it is instinctual for them to hit the ball there. It wasn't that they were trying to be rude, it was just how they had learned to practice as little girls in the ghetto of Compton, CA.

When warm-up time was over, Richard called the girls over to the net, where he was standing. I began to walk over to hear the instructions for the match, but this time Richard stopped me.

"Dave, this is a private family meeting," he said.

"Okay, I'll pick up the balls," I replied.

I started retrieving the balls we had used in our drills, but I was still in earshot of most everything that was said. Whenever Richard gave me the line, 'It's a family matter' or 'family meeting', I knew he was up to something. He began by informing the girls of how important this match had become. He said that he wanted them to have fun out there and give the people an entertaining match. He started to say something else and then looked over at me to see if I was paying attention. I walked away, towards the back fence, as he gave the girls further instructions that I was unable to hear.

When he finished talking with the girls, he motioned me to come over. "Dave I'm going to need you to sit in our other box for this match. We have the owner of the Puma Corporation flying in from Germany today to watch Serena play," he said.

Richard had control of who sat in the main box (A) for each match, the box he always sat in, and since this match was going to be televised nationally, he probably didn't want me to get any more airtime than he was going to get. It was disappointing for me, because the day before, I had done a little marketing for myself with the help of my sister, Charlotte. We had locked down a sponsorship deal with Bollé sunglasses, which was good for the Lipton finals only. The contract was done so last minute, that the details were written on the back of a business card and then signed by both parties. The deal specified that for every camera shot I got during the finals, showing me wearing the Bollé sunglasses, I would receive five hundred dollars. So with all the attention Richard had been luring to the box with his crazy signs, I figured I was assured at least a half dozen camera shots. I felt that I had done a good job in my first attempt at getting a new sponsorship deal. Never before had I sought out sponsorship. Usually, whoever Venus signed with, I would sign with also. I did not realize how many companies were out there, chomping at the bit for exposure linked to the Williams sisters. With time running out, my sister set up another meeting with Rado, a title sponsor of the tournament. They quickly offered me free product, but said it would take a few weeks for any kind of an endorsement deal. They hoped I would wear their logo hat at the finals, but I had already promised the Wilson representatives that I would wear their hat in the finals. Wilson had thrown in a set of their new fat shaft golf clubs to secure a sponsorship deal, so they were number one in my book. All I could promise Rado was that I would wear their watch. The Rado representatives happily agreed to the deal, and I became a walking billboard, with as many sponsors as an Indy 500 racecar.

When I got the bump by Richard from box A to box B, it killed my chances of getting the multitude of camera shots I had envisioned for the Bollé deal. In fact, box B did not get any TV time. Without Richard and his signs, dancing, and flag waving, there was no show for the cameras and no story for the announcers. Box B was dead air. I guess I should have brought my own signs, or maybe hired a dancing purple dinosaur to bring some attention to box B. Nevertheless, there was still a tennis match to be played, and I still had a job to do. From then on, I would leave the self-marketing antics to Richard, and just take my notes for my tournament report.

The 1999 Lipton final was the tournament that birthed the scandalous rumor that Richard had fixed the results of matches between Venus and Serena. At the Lipton, Venus did have more to lose because she was the defending champion, which meant she had to defend her previous year's points in order to maintain her ranking. At the time, most people felt that Serena was playing the better of the two sisters, especially considering the fact that she had just come off consecutive tournament victories at Paris and Indian Wells. Two valid reasons for anyone to get suspicious, but it was reaching.

In the match, Serena came out tight and Venus steam-rolled her 6-1 in the first set. After that, I found myself rooting for Serena because she was the underdog. She would occasionally look up to box B, and I would pump my fist at her and yell encouragement. Although I was encouraging Serena, deep down I knew Venus was going to win. I expected a straight set victory however, and was very surprised at how Venus played in the second set. Compared to the first set, she almost looked as though she was playing in slow motion, and she had a rash of unforced errors that allowed Serena to win the second set 6-4.

After the set, Richard was up in the box holding a sign that read 'Welcome to the Williams Show.' Richard's ego was engulfing the stadium as he danced around in Box A. With his signs, he seemed to be saying, "see what I have orchestrated!" The crowd had been cheering for a third set, and they got what they wanted. One set to see which Williams was the best. They were keeping the crowd entertained, as instructed by Richard.

Venus played the third set much like the first, showing her powerful, more mature game and was no match for her younger sister. She went on to win the third set 6-4 and remained the Lipton champion. There was an emotional and touching hug at the net instead of the traditional handshake, and I felt proud as I watched them share their sisterly love in front of the world. It was a historic WTA match, as it was the first all sisters final in 115 years. There had only been one other in 1884 at Wimbledon.

So was the match fixed? Did Richard tell Serena to lose? The question grew louder and stronger after the sisters met again at the 2000 Wimbledon semifinal. In that match, Venus won in straight sets, with Serena double faulting on match point. Like the Lipton match, Serena was deemed the one to beat, the better player. At Wimbledon, Serena had dominated her first five rounds, winning all of them in straight sets. She had only lost fifteen games in the whole tournament.

She had dished out breadsticks and bagels (6-1=breadstick/6-0=bagel) to four of her opponents, showing that she had a more experienced grass court game. But once again, her superior play was stopped by older sister Venus. Some say that because Serena had already won a grand slam title (1999 U.S. Open), it was Venus's turn to win. It was Serena's tears of distress after the match and in the post match press conference that led some to believe that she was upset, not at losing, but at not being allowed to win.

So, did I think the fix was on? That was the big question, John Clark, the sports caster for NBC channel five news in West Palm Beach, Florida called to ask me. He sent a camera crew out to my club for comment and then called me into the station for a live Wimbledon recap, each time hoping to unveil some proof to the scandalous rumors. However, all I could do was repeat what I had already said to numerous other reporters. Remember who I said would always win when the sisters played each other? Venus. And didn't Venus win both those matches? Yes. Now, did Richard tell Serena to lose the Wimbledon semifinal? This I could not tell you. I will say however, that I would not put it past him. In all my years with Richard, I've noticed how he loved to see just how far he could push the envelope with people. He has publicly announced that he was going to buy the Rockefeller Center and that he owned air space in India. The National Enquirer stated, in an interview with a nephew living with the Williams' and with a former lover of Richard's, that Richard told them that he gave Serena specific instructions to let Venus win the Wimbledon semifinal. If that were true, it would be the biggest scandal to hit the sports world since the White Sox fixed the World Series in 1919. The WTA would have no choice but to suspend both Venus and Serena and possibly ban them from the tour indefinitely, in order to save their credibility. Richard would also be banned from coaching on the tour and there would have to be prize money returned and fines levied. However, there was really no way to prove the allegations, as they were all based on hearsay. When reporters addressed the issue, Richard's ego was bruised, and he flew off the handle, saying: "It's a God damn shame that people come up with that bullshit! When McEnroe and his brother played, when Chris Evert and her sister played, no one asked about that!" In my opinion, there are two reasons that no one asked the question back then. First, one brother and one sister were clearly better than the other, whereas Venus and Serena were much closer in ability. Second, the father's of McEnroe and Evert were not making outlandish statements to the media or manipulating their way around the tour. The fact that Richard had been known to exaggerate to the point of lying gave him the best alibi. If you were to go up to a WTA official today and say, "Do you know what Richard Williams just told me?" They would probably just roll their eyes and go about their day. To say that he had lost credibility over the years is an understatement. The past champions of the WTA, the tennis hierarchy, and all the tennis fans around the world can only hope that their sport has not been taken advantage of and corrupted in such a way as the rumors implied.

Every player, on both the men and women's tour, has a handful of interesting tournament stories and maybe even a scandal or two to his or her name. How can they not? Today's best players live an almost rock star lifestyle. Traveling the world, signing autographs for thousands of fans, and attending player and sponsor parties with the world's rich and famous, is all part of a typical week in the lives of top tennis players. Multiply that week by ten, and you will have an idea of a typical week on tour for Venus and Serena. They have reached celebrity status that extends well beyond the tennis world. A week for them might include, a spot on the tonight show with Jay Leno or late night with David Letterman, a production of TV commercials for one of their sponsors, a photo shoot for a popular magazine, a spot in a game show, and an appearance as presenter at a celebrity awards event. They receive so much more attention than most players, and with the tennis circuit being so demanding, one might think that all that extra attention would be a strain. It could be, but Venus and Serena have been in that celebrity spotlight since I met them in 1992. According to them, it is just part of being a great player and they deserve all of it.

THE
RIDE
ENDS

XXX

As with any great roller coaster ride, once you reach the top there is nowhere to go but down. Some drops are gradual, bringing a smile to your face as the wind blows through your hair. Other drops are fierce and sharp, injecting terror throughout your body and producing screams of sheer panic as you hurl towards the ground. My roller coaster ride with the Williams sisters had endured many ups and downs and now, at the 1999 U.S. Open, it had reached its pinnacle.

During the two months prior to the U.S. Open, Richard was like the invisible man. He had not returned any of my phone calls to schedule practices, regarding tournament travel or about receiving my promised bonuses. There were no letters or emails about renewing our coaching agreement for the upcoming season and there was no itinerary for the U.S. Open, which was scheduled to be my last tournament to attend with Venus and Serena as their hitting coach. Two days before the U.S. Open, I finally reached Richard on his cell phone. He quickly brushed me off, saying he was in a meeting with some people from Microsoft and that I should call him back in one hour and twelve minutes. An interesting time slot, but nothing I hadn't grown accustomed to over the years. When I called Richard back he answered, and immediately began the brush off routine again. I cut him off because I needed answers to a few questions I had, concerning the U.S. Open. I quickly asked him the questions I had written down in my notebook before he could think of another reason to hang up on me.

"I have the U.S. Open as the last tournament Venus wanted me to attend. Is Venus playing?" I asked.

"Venus won't be playing," Richard answered. "She's going to be in school." Richard always used the education line on people when he wanted to give a quick answer. I think he figured that most people would commend him for his views on education. By saying school was more important than tennis, I think he believed that he was better than any other tennis father/parent. I knew better though, and on my paper I wrote down his real answer as, 'Yes, Venus is playing the U.S. Open'.

Next, I asked, "Since Venus and Serena are traveling so much and are not able to practice here in Florida, do you want me to start traveling full-time?"

"We will have to have a family meeting tonight and I will let you know tomorrow. I would like you to pick up a passport as soon as possible though," he said.

For that answer I wrote, 'Don't expect a call tomorrow and he will be doing all the traveling and coaching'.

"Would you like me to hit with Serena at the Open, since Venus won't be going?" was my next question.

"I would like you to be on call. In fact, when you get to New York, call my cell phone and leave your phone numbers," he answered.

I had already given him my hotel information with phone number and addresses two months ago, so my interpretation of that answer read, 'He won't be taking his cell phone to New York, so when I call he won't be available'. I had become very good at interpreting Richard's statements over the years.

I arrived at the U.S. Open a day before the main draw started. I had an interview set up with a reporter from Sports Illustrated, who wanted the inside story of the guy who had been hitting with Venus and Serena all these years. The reporter said that his article was for Sports Illustrated for Women edition, and that as a special U.S. Open segment, it would be on the Internet the following day or two. In the interview, I talked as much as I could about the girls' games and how well they were playing coming into the U.S. Open. However, the reporter wanted more. He asked about Richard, the family and if I was going to coach the girls full-time. All I could tell him at the time was that my name was in the hat if Richard was going to step away, but off the record I told him that Richard's ego would never let that happen. "He has told me time and time again that he was a better coach than any coach you could think of: Gilbert, Roche, Solomon, Bollettieri, etc..." I said.

After the interview, I did a photo shoot with a Sports Illustrated photographer out by court number eleven on the U.S. Open grounds, and then I went straight to the practice courts to find Richard, Venus, or Serena. Venus and Serena were just coming off practice court number one as I arrived. I had to holler at them through the gate since I did not yet have my credentials to roam freely about. Venus heard me and immediately stopped and came over. We had not seen each other in two months because she had been traveling all around the globe. She was smiling big as she walked up and I slipped by the autograph seekers and the gate attendant to give her a big hug. I congratulated her on her latest tournament win over Davenport and she told me, "I've got Davenport's number now." I told her I would be at her match the next night and if she wanted to hit, to call me on my cell. She said she would call and then Richard walked up. He whispered something to Venus and she turned and walked into the locker rooms.

"Hi Dave," Richard said. He gave me the usual hug and asked how I felt. After a little small talk, I asked Richard if I could get credentials for the week, since I was going to be on call. He reached into his pocket and pulled out a stack of tickets.

"We don't have anymore passes Dave, but here's some tickets for the week," he said. There was no mention of the fact that Venus was playing the tournament instead of attending school as he had told me earlier. He seemed elusive to answer any of my questions about practice times for the week, and when I asked him about the fact that he had not paid me in six months, he got angry.

"The check should be on its way," was his only reply.

It was such an insignificant amount, compared to what the girls were now bringing in each week, that his reaction to my asking convinced me to the fattened size of his ever-growing ego. Getting paid over the last year had been a hassle. Richard had to have Venus or Serena write out my checks, because it seemed he just could not part with his money. I got that feeling you get inside your stomach just as the roller coaster is about to make its biggest plunge. Just then, a car pulled up and the driver yelled, "Williams!" "That's my car Dave," Richard said, "I have to go meet with the mayor." He shook my hand and said we would have to talk later. As I watched the car pull away, I knew that we probably would not talk again. I felt the ride was ending for me, but it really would not be over until I heard Venus say it was over.

The following night, I attended Venus's match on stadium court. This was the first time in five years that I had watched one of Venus's matches from a seat other than in the player's boxes. It was not the same. The player's box was a special place to a player on the court. As the emotions of the match unfold, players look to their box to share their joy, admit their frustrations, or to seek support from their family, coaches and friends. Being in any other seat meant missing out on all those emotional expressions. Venus was very emotional and her looks of distress, agony, and joy always made me feel like I was a part of her matches. Serena was more stone faced throughout her matches and usually only showed anger or pain.

Venus won her match easily, and I decided to watch the first set of the next match and then go to the transportation desk to see if I could catch up with Venus before she left for her hotel. Since I knew her post match routine, I figured it would take about forty minutes before she would be ready to leave. When I arrived just outside the transportation area, Venus was talking to Alexandra Stevenson, another young player on the WTA tour, while they waited on a car. Since the transportation area was located outside the fences, I would have to leave the tournament grounds to go talk with Venus. I walked outside the gates and up to Venus, smiling as always and expecting her to extend her hand or give me some other sort of greeting. Instead, she turned away from me and continued her conversation. I put my hand on her shoulder from behind and said, "Great match Venus." She pulled away from my hand and said, "Oh, thanks," and then continued to talk with Alexandra Stevenson as they walked towards an approaching car. While the driver of the car was busy loading Venus's bags, she turned towards me, making eye contact. She smiled with her head tilted and turned her palms up as if to say, 'sorry Dave, I can't talk to you'. She then got in her car and left.

I walked back towards the gate, bewildered and baffled at how Venus's demeanor towards me had changed overnight. The roller coaster ride was definitely over the top and on its way downward, and I no longer had the strength to stop it. I had been through so many ups and downs with the Williams' over the last seven years that I was too exhausted mentally and physically to keep pursuing the ride or playing the games. I probably could have pushed all the right buttons to keep the ride going, but it would not have lasted much longer anyway. I could not feed Richards ego on a daily basis anymore. He was no longer 'good ole Richard', who appreciated my efforts, now he was, 'King Richard', which is what he liked to call himself, who demanded more, gave less and didn't have time for anyone who wasn't throwing money or attention at him. It was obvious that Richard had decided that he did not need my help anymore. There was never going to be any contract, which he had dangled in front of me for years. The girls had learned all the strokes and shots they needed, and all that remained, was to execute those shots and strokes within a game plan. Since there was no chance of him letting me travel full-time, the girls would have to learn how to construct a winning game plan on their own.

When I got to the gate to re-enter the U.S. Open grounds, the attendant stopped me and informed me that I would have to buy another ticket to get inside. So, not only was I felling a little low from Venus's brush off, but now I was also shut out of the U.S. Open grounds at 10pm without a ride. I took the number seven train back to Manhattan, thinking the whole time of the night's incidents and wondering if I should just 'Fade Away', as my friend Angel sings, or if I should try harder to appease 'King Richard' and keep the roller coaster going?

XXXI

As I walked into my hotel room at the Parker Meridian, the phone rang. I answered, hoping that it might be Venus or Serena calling to schedule a hit for the following day or explain what was going on.

"Hello, this is Dave," I answered.

The man's voice on the other end said, "I don't want you around Venus or Serena. Leave now or go in a body bag."

"Who is this?" I asked.

"You should be more careful where you leave your phone," he said.

I had lost my cell phone, or so I thought, the night before when I was out having a drink with a friend at a restaurant in Manhattan. I thought I had left it on the bar, but when I went back to retrieve it, the restaurant said there was no phone found. This guy must have been at the restaurant. My mind raced through all the faces I had seen standing nearby me. I hung up the phone and called hotel security. This was the third time I'd been threatened, but the first time someone had gone so far as to take something from me. I had chalked the first two threats up to jealousy, but his one, being as it was in New York, had a more penetrating effect on me. A security agent arrived at my door ten minutes later and I explained the situation.

I stayed low for the rest of the tournament, only going to the day matches. I switched hotels and rode the player's transportation to the site each day, staying out of the underground subway system. I canceled my phone and made travel arrangements on the first flight out after the women's final. Venus and Serena were both in the semifinals and the chance of an all Williams final would have been the perfect ending to my Williams roller coaster ride.

Venus played Hingis in her semifinal, and it was the most competitive match I had ever watched Venus play. She had become such a fierce competitor in 1999 and it showed in her eyes as she played. A much different look than the 'wide-eyed deer in the headlights' look that she had had in her first U.S. Open in 1997.

Venus lost the first set 6-1, making too many unforced errors, but she cleaned up her strokes in the second set and ran Hingis to the four corners of the court to win the set 6-4. At a set apiece, both players were running at top speed, exchanging blows like two prizefighters of contrasting styles. Venus's determination was the best I had ever seen. She would later say that her game was not on, but that did not stop her from giving her all. The New York crowd loved the effort from both players, and every point in the third set produced a roar of applause. Some points were so long, expending each player so much energy, that when the point was over, both bent at the waist to catch their breath, not knowing who had just won it. In the end, after an epic battle, Hingis had won a spot in the finals. Hingis looked paste-faced as she approached Venus at the net. Venus had put her into oxygen debt throughout most of the third set by getting every ball back, and minus a few errors, it could have easily been Venus moving on to the finals to face her sister Serena.

Serena had beaten Davenport in the semifinals 6-4, 1-6, 6-4 and now faced Hingis in the finals, a match I was not about to miss. Could Serena do what Venus could not in 1997? Serena dominated Hingis in the finals, winning in straight sets 6-3, 7-6. The match turned out to be much less dramatic than Venus's semifinal. It was obvious that Hingis was still feeling the ill effects of her match with Venus. Serena played great, but in my opinion, you have to give Venus a big fat assist, as she beat Hingis to a pulp before losing to her. To Serena's credit, she dominated Hingis in the winner department, hitting thirty-six winners - twenty-nine more than Hingis. Serena attacked at every opportunity and showed how overpowering her game had become since turning pro.

The power of winning flooded Serena with a sea of mixed emotions. On match point, as a Hingis's ball sailed long, Serena raised her hands to her chest and mouthed the words, "Oh my God, I won, Oh my God." She did not know how to react. This was the biggest win of her short career! Later, in the press conference, she told the media,

"It was pretty exciting. I'm thinking, Should I scream? Should I yell? Should I cry? What should I do? I guess I ended up doing them all."

I must have jumped ten feet on match point. Serena was so happy, and I was happy for her. She had just done something that big sister Venus could never do as long as she lived and that was to become the first African-American female in the Open era and the first Williams girl to win the U.S. Open singles title. It was what both Venus and Serena had been working for their whole lives, and it was what I had spent the last seven years in hopes to see. Needless to say, it was a joyous time for all. Almost.

Venus had her head buried beneath a hood throughout most of Serena's match. I knew she must have been very disappointed that it was not her out there playing her sister, and as I looked over at her in the player's box, trying whole heartedly to celebrate along with Serena, I could not help but feel sad for Venus. I wished I could have been beside her to help console her, but someone else would have to make that connection with Venus now that I was not there. She was sad and there was disappointment, but it was not because Serena had won, it was because she was not happy about how she had played in her semifinal. Serena even said that she was inspired to try harder because of how Venus felt about her semifinal match. "She was really down," Serena said. "That really encouraged me to be even tougher out there." Venus would have to find a way to get past the disappointment if she was ever going to win a grand slam title. To make the 1999 U.S. Open even sweeter for Serena and maybe less disappointing for Venus, they won the doubles title, defeating Chanda Rubin and Sandrine Testud 4-6, 6-1, 6-4.

I did not see Venus, Serena, or any of the Williams' for the rest of 1999. After numerous phone calls and emails, it was apparent that no one was going to return my calls or letters. My presence at practices was replaced by mediocre hitters, who could barely sustain a rally with

Serena, and who could not hold their own against Venus's power. My sources informed me that Venus was not happy with the changes and that she had not even played since losing in the semifinals in Moscow in mid-October. With all the changes in her routine, the disappointment of the 1999 U.S. Open still unsettled within her, and some personal problems at home, she was unmotivated. Then, just before the 2000 season was about to begin, it was reported that she had tendonitis in both her wrists. Venus was hurting both mentally and physically and in a similar fashion to me, her roller coaster ride was heading downward fast.

The start of the 2000 season saw Venus on the sidelines for almost four months. The rumor was out at the Key Biscayne tournament that Venus was contemplating retirement. As I walked the grounds of the tournament, my cell phone rang. It was a reporter from Sports Illustrated. "Dave, is it true that Venus is going to retire?" he asked. I said that I had not heard that rumor and that I figured it to be a publicity stunt dawned by Richard Williams himself. "If Venus did not say it, I would not believe it." I said. She was too much of a competitor to retire at the age of nineteen. "She will be back," I said, "I just can't tell you where or when."

Venus did come back, making her start to 2000 in Hamburg, Germany on may 1st. She showed up with a new look. The full headdress of beads that had been her trademark look since before her pro debut in 1994 was gone. In its place was a new hairdo, featuring only a few beads and a much longer hair length. She also had both wrists taped, showing the world the pain she had gone through and maybe hoping for a little sympathy instead of criticism for her absence from the tour. She looked thinner, lacking the muscle mass that had intimidated opponents in previous years and her strokes were rusty. She used her first three tournaments as a warm-up tuning her strokes and learning to compete again. Once she got her timing back and her conditioning improved, she turned her disastrous first half of 2000 into the best second half year of her career. First, she won Wimbledon, beating long time foe Lindsay Davenport. The tournament Venus had once said to me was the one tournament she wanted to win the most was now hers. Her elation on match point showed, as she jumped and twirled her way to the net. All the troubles and disappointments that she had been shouldering since the 1999 U.S. Open were lifted away and once again, she was the great player that the hype had always predicted she would be.

The next day, as if to return the favor for easing her pain at last year's U.S. Open, Venus helped get Serena the doubles title. Again, the Williams girls had dominated a grand slam event and again they had made history. Venus became the first African-American since Althea Gibson to win the Wimbledon singles title and Venus and Serena together became the first sisters in history to each win a grand slam singles title. Venus was definitely back and she was on a roll. She won her next tournament at Stanford and then two more, San Diego and New Haven. By the time she got to the U.S. Open, she had a twenty-two match-winning streak. All that time off had made her hungry to compete. She attacked the 2000 U.S. Open like a tigress, reaching the semifinals where she would have a rematch against last year's spoiler, Martina Hingis. The first set went to Hingis and the second to Venus.

Hingis jumped to a 5-3 lead in the final set and was up 30-0 on her serve. The next point was more about destiny than tennis. Hingis approached the net on a good approach shot that forced Venus to throw up a lob that did not even make it to the service line. Hingis would normally hit that lob for a winner every time, but this time she hit a mediocre shot that Venus chased down and hit a backhand for a winner. Venus's past U.S. Open disappointments evaporated on that single laser-like backhand shot. It was her turn to win and she knew it.

She erased Hingis's break to tie the match at 5-5, then played two flawless games to win the set and the match 4-6, 6-3, 7-5. Venus was happy, but calmly celebrated. Her eyes told me the story once again. She was focused on the title and no one would stop her this time. Venus went on to beat Davenport in the finals 6-4, 7-5. Although her ranking did not show it, Venus was the best player in the world and had been since Wimbledon. It was her second U.S. Open final in only her fourth attempt and it was her second grand slam title in a row. What could top that?

There was a new event to the tour in 2000, the Olympics. Venus barely had time to celebrate her U.S. Open victory because she and Serena had to fly to Sydney, Australia to help represent the United States in the 2000 Olympic games. Venus was playing in the singles competition with fellow Americans Monica Seles and Lindsay Davenport and in the doubles competition with sister Serena. Venus was unbeaten in singles since losing at the French Open in early June and her consecutive match winning streak was the longest since Hingis won thirty-seven in 1997. In front of a sell out crowd, Venus put the cherry on top of her year by beating Elena Dementieva 6-2, 6-4, thereby clinching an Olympic gold medal. She backed that victory up with another gold medal performance the following day in the doubles event with Serena. When receiving their gold medals, Venus was a little overwhelmed by her performance. "I felt really emotional. You see it on TV. It was really great," she said. "It was me!" Venus's roller coaster tennis career had reached yet another peak, and Serena's was once again climbing fast. Together, the sisters had accomplished more in their short careers than most players could ever hope to achieve. What had started as a father's dream on the glass filled, gang-controlled tennis courts of Compton, CA, had become a reality on the grass, clay, and hard courts of the world. But what if Venus and Serena had not won? What if, like Kournikova, they had showed potential but not greatness? Would it all have been worth it for me? I guess for some people that might be a hard question to answer. Most of my friends did not think it would have been worth it for them. The death threats alone were reason enough to abandon the ride. Tack on the self-discipline to stay in top physical shape, the mental anguish and manipulation, not receiving any credit publicly for the help in developing Venus and Serena's games, and finally to be let go without any kind of a thank you from any of the Williams family. Was it all worth it?

In the years that have followed those 'seven years', I have watched Venus and Serena play numerous times. I still root for the girls and find that I still get butterflies in my stomach when they have break points against them or squander away match points. If it is said that imitation is the highest form of compliment, then each time I watch them hit one of my shots, I have to feel good about the hours of hitting I had with them. I have been able to re-live many of the stories that were memorable to me while writing this book. I realize my ride with Venus and Serena may not have been a path that everyone would have taken, but for me it was the only path. As a young boy, I had a dream to become a successful coach and although I made it to my destination, it was the journey that I truly enjoyed. I hope that anyone who reads this book understands that there are no guarantees in life of fulfilling one's dreams, but with self-discipline and a relentless pursuit of those dreams, you too may enjoy the ride. I feel proud at what great champions Venus and Serena have become, but my proudest moment came, not when I was coaching them, but at the 2001 U.S. Open. Venus and Serena dominated the field and both reached the finals. It was the first time in history that two sisters would face each other in a U.S. Open final, and the first time two African-Americans would play in a grand slam final. The sister rivalry that currently had Venus up four matches to Serena's one, had taken center stage and primetime live. For the first time ever, the women's final would be played at night, 8pm on primetime TV. In every way imaginable, the match was historic. Although, Venus won 6-2, 6-4 in just sixty-nine minutes, it was obvious to everyone watching that these two sisters, who grew up playing on the crack filled courts of Compton, CA, were the best in the world. After the final ball was struck, Venus and Serena met at the net and showed the world that it was family and being a true best friend that mattered most. Venus put aside the celebrating and gloating of her victory as she approached Serena. She had something else to tell her little sister, something no other opponent would ever hear. It wasn't the usual, nice try, or good effort, or thanks that Venus had to say to the sister who had been there with her through all the ups and downs of her career. No, Venus had a much more emotional heart felt phrase for her kid sister, and as they embraced at the net, Venus told her, "I love you." That was my proudest moment.

I now spend my days teaching and coaching players of all ages and abilities, keeping an eye out for that next tennis phenom, who might start the roller coaster ride all over again. So was it all worth it? "Excuse me, I hear the tennis pro shop phone ringing and I wouldn't want to miss the call."

VENUS WILLIAMS GRAND SLAM HIGHLIGHTS

	2001	2000	1999	1998	1997
AUSTRALIAN OPEN	SF	---	QF	QF	---
FRENCH OPEN	1R	QF	4R	QF	2R
WIMBLEDON	WIN	WIN	QF	QF	1R
U.S. OPEN	WIN	WIN	SF	SF	FLS

CAREER DOUBLES HIGHLIGHTS (WITH SERENA):
8 TITLES: 2001 Australian Open, 2000 Wimbledon, 2000 Olympics, 1999 French Open, 1999 U.S. Open, 1999 Hanover, 1998 Oklahoma City, 1998 Zurich

FINALIST: 1999 San Diego

CAREER MIXED DOUBLES HIGHLIGHTS:
(WITH J. GIMELSTOB)
2 TITLES: 1998 Australian Open, 1998 French Open
FINALIST: 1998 Wimbledon

ADDITIONAL FACTS:
United States Fed Cup team member 1995, 1999.
United States Olympic team member 2000.

WTA SEASON-ENDING RANKING:
2001- , 2000-#3, 1999-#3, 1998-#5, 1997-#22, 1996-#204, 1995-#204

SERENA WILLIAMS GRAND SLAM HIGHLIGHTS

	2001	2000	1999	1998	1997
AUSTRALIAN OPEN	QF	4R	3R	2R	---
FRENCH OPEN	QF	---	3R	4R	---
WIMBLEDON	QF	SF	---	3R	---
U.S. OPEN	FINAL	QF	WIN	3R	---

CAREER DOUBLES HIGHLIGHTS (WITH VENUS):
8 TITLES: 2001 Australian Open, 2000 Wimbledon, 2000 Olympics, 1999 French Open, 1999 U.S. Open, 1999 Hanover, 1998 Oklahoma City, 1998 Zurich

FINALIST: 1999 San Diego

CAREER MIXED DOUBLES HIGHLIGHTS:
(WITH M. MYRNI)
2 TITLES: 1998 WIMBLEDON, 1998 U.S. OPEN
FINALIST: 1999 AUSTRALIAN OPEN

(WITH L. LOBO)
FINALIST: 1998 FRENCH OPEN

ADDITIONAL FACTS:
United States Fed Cup team member 1999.
United States Olympic team member 2000.

WTA SEASON-ENDING RANKING:
2001-#7 , 2000-#6, 1999-#4, 1998-#20, 1997-#99